Memorial Library

THE FIRST PRESBYTERIAN CHURCH
4785 Shankland Road - Willoughby, Ohio

GIFT OF
George B. McClellan

RELIGIOUS BUILDINGS FOR TODAY

RELIGIOUS BUILDINGS FOR TODAY

Edited by John Knox Shear, AIA
Editor-in-Chief, *Architectural Record*

An Architectural Record Book
Published by F. W. Dodge Corporation

FOREWORD

The building-committee member who professes little knowledge of architecture and of the architectural implications of his own way of worship is not rare; he is about as frequent a phenomenon as the man who "knows what he likes"; and is, in sad truth, often one and the same.

The churches and temples in this book were designed by architects in cooperation with committeemen and religious leaders who may have known what they liked but were not dogmatic about it. No presumption or prejudice obscured the opportunity to approach — if not always to achieve — the quality of architecture which their faiths and their communities deserved. Buildings in the explicit services of God — like any buildings housing activities of high regard — demand the best talent and the best thinking, the broadest approach and the most intense prosecution.

Although the people who were concerned in these buildings shared the conservatism inherent in all committees and must have dreaded risking what at first might seem bizarre to some, they appear generally to have dreaded even more the kind of dismal design that develops out of fear, and poverty of spirit, and untrammeled sentimentality. While there are in these examples great differences, there are great common denominators as well. None could have been achieved without the encouragement and the enthusiasm of informed and interested committees working with inspired designers.

All of the buildings presented here, and the several essays on religious building problems, were first published in recent issues of Architectural Record. They were intended — at the very least — as a report to architect and engineer readers on developments in religious-building programming, design, and construction. Actually they have proved, in the hands of the design profession, effective instruments in broadening the horizons of building-committee members faced with the enormous responsibility of formulating a clear expression of a congregation's aspirations in such a way as to inspire rather than intimidate the design. That they have been of significant help in repeated specific instances, as well as useful in stimulating general awareness of religious design possibilities, may be attributed to both the quality and the range of examples chosen.

A great variety of faiths, of sites, of budgets, of program requirements, structural methods, and attitudes are represented here, but above all, a great variety of design characteristics; for, though the common thread of good design unites all these examples, each achieves unique character through the modifying influences of a particular architect, a particular congregation, and a particular set of circumstances. It is a broad selection, but not so broad as to include the banal or the bad.

To the building committees, architects, engineers, and artists, who have patiently and prayerfully made these buildings possible we owe a real debt, just as we do to all those who have written here of worship and design and the unity which through talent and humility may be achieved in them. The ideas stated here in words and images recommend this book for all who are concerned with re-establishing the vitality of three-dimensional religious expression in their communities and with re-establishing the leadership of the church and the temple in the arts.

John Knox Shear

March 7, 1957

CONTENTS

THE DESIGN OF CHURCHES

For three generations the depressing effect of bad architecture has been visited upon the worshipers of America. Because our church buildings have seldom appealed to our total interests, they have failed to satisfy us. It must be acknowledged that churches share this failure with other building types, but because they are churches the failure seems more poignant.

Most of our buildings have failed because they have not been drawn from and do not express the whole range of man's needs and the experiences which are constantly reshaping those needs. Our buildings are, rather, the expression of our interest in certain fragments of experience, in selected stimuli. At best it is difficult to treat with the whole of any problem. Architects are not alone in their tendency to overlook the evidence of man's total experience in favor of working with those experiences and ideas which happen to be particularly stimulating at the moment. Dealing with parts of experience and parts of ideas is easier. Moreover, by changing periodically the particular set of motivations the illusion of progress may be achieved. It is easier to organize building form if one eliminates many of the considerations which should normally influence form.

Ralph Adams Cram wanted us to shut out of sight and out of mind all our experience since Gothic. Today's architects are little different from yesterday's. We are simply motivated by a different set of exclusive stimuli. It is a rare architect today who is able to resist the fascination of concentrating his interest on a favorite material, shape or system of construction. Too often it is a predominantly intellectual fascination and as such necessarily fatal for the total interests of the people.

For architecture is an art which is apprehended sensually. It is a spatial art whose point of departure is utility and in which vision is the triggering sense. When the spatial and visual solutions to our utilitarian problems can be solved in such a way as to appeal also to our minds, we may achieve an architecture that will satisfy the spirit. But an architecture which tries to appeal to our minds without satisfying our senses or accommodating our activities can never be more than a partially utilitarian, highly personal kind of sculpture.

That is where we are today, but we need not remain there. We have still the opportunity to focus first on the spatial, then the structural; on the sensual before the rational. Surely our best interests are served through concentration on those things which have the most pertinence for man and hence — architecture.

In the design of churches the need for a direction of interests which can be shared with clergy, church officials and building committees is more than ever imperative today. Church membership is growing at a rate faster than the population. The buildings demanded by both new and expanding congregations must provide for the whole family throughout the entire week. A much larger proportion of the building budget must be used for educational, recreational and social facilities. New structural methods, new mechanical systems, and new equipment of all kinds must be employed in order to fit the budget and the program and to compete with the attractions of secular activities. Finally a growing interest in the historical meanings of our ways of worship and their relationship to the architecture and art of our churches is forcing the reexamination of the appropriateness of the spatial and visual organizations which we have inherited from the very recent past.

These are relatively new and tremendously challenging determinants. Architects can meet these challenges. If they will, we can look forward once again to a significant architecture. There are signs of it even now and when added to the handful of good churches of the past ten years, there is cause for encouragement. On the pages following there is apparent evidence of architects' concern for how people use buildings and how they respond to them.

ON GETTING GOOD ARCHITECTURE FOR THE CHURCH

How to get good architecture for the church is not an academic question. More church buildings are being erected than ever before and there is every prospect that the tempo of construction will increase. In being concerned with good architecture for the church, therefore, we are not dealing with a hypothetical issue. We are faced with immediate concerns — construction today which should have architectural and religious validity for tomorrow.

My interest in good architecture for the church derives from my concern that the Church truly witness its faith in the 20th century. While the Church has made enormous efforts in education, in social action, in psychology and pastoral care, the Church has been negligent in the arts and in worship.

Because we have allowed our best traditions in worship to decay and because our tradition with respect to the arts has been one of suspicion, Protestants, at least, have not had a living tradition on which to draw. Fortunately, growing interest in the arts and worship holds promise of renewal in the future. But these are years in which fateful decisions influencing future generations are being made. Although I do not write as a professional in architecture and the allied arts, I write out of a conviction that new insights in worship and the arts are already available to us. I write out of some awareness of the new directions in Christian thought and out of a concern that church architecture not shadow the past but anticipate the future.

Unfortunately, we are burdened in the churches with a baleful legacy of misunderstanding, romanticism, and ignorance about the question of architecture for the church. As far as I can recall, my instruction in one of the country's leading centers of theological training never dealt with the problem except insofar as we were led to believe that in the interests of worship the Congregational churches, for whose ministry we were preparing, should look to Episcopal churches as their architectural ideal. We were nurtured in the belief there was a "holy" style for the church and a "secular" style suitable for a factory or a school or even a home.

Double standard architecture

But one of the basic problems which confronts a local church planning to erect a new building is the breach between architecture for the church and architecture for the rest of society. The hiatus between architecture for the church and architecture for other institutions and groups in society exposes the shallowness of our understanding of the Gospel and its relevance to all areas of our common life and all realms of society. The continuing penchant among many churches for Gothic and Renaissance denies their assertion that Christianity has significance for all aspects of man's life. It is an architectural denial of the meaning of the Incarnation and the belief that God continues to speak his Word in the language of each new age.

The failure to face architectural facts started in the 19th century. Soon after the Industrial Revolution and the emergence of new technological devices, eclecticism commenced to exert its influence. By returning to the past we shall be saved. The Oxford movement in England and the Cambridge Camden Society with its ritual and ceremonial concerns spurred the return to the past. The Gothic "style" came to be considered the only architecture consonant with the spiritual meanings perceived in the restoration of pre-Reformation ceremonial and ritual.

The Gothic mask

The early Victorians covered the machine in their shame. Perhaps they confused the ruthlessness of 19th-century industrial society with the new techniques and the new materials — concrete, cast iron, and later, steel. At any rate, it was not only the churches which were designed as miniature Gothic cathedrals, but factories, warehouses, and railroad stations were made to appear like medieval castles, fortifications, and cathedrals. The revival of Gothic architecture, I believe, enabled a people to ignore the injustices of a rapidly expanding empire by escaping romantically into a past which they neither understood nor could enter.

On the positive side, the vogue of Gothic in the Victorian era became a form of social protest by architects, poets, and seers. Their motivation was often religiously prophetic, but they failed to grapple with their age.

Despite the peril of appearing chauvinistic, I believe

BY MARVIN HALVERSON

**Executive Director, Department of
Worship and the Arts,
National Council of Churches**

there is an American tradition in architecture from which the church can learn about its failure in the past and its present opportunity. Although modern architecture is indebted to many 19th-century Europeans and reached a degree of maturity in 20th-century Europe, modern architecture is strikingly indebted to American influences. Lewis Mumford has suggested that the Yankee clipper ship and the American ax, and I would add, the New England frame meeting house, were forms which in their honest treatment of materials and their direct relationship to purpose were things of beauty. This tradition of integrity flowered again when from 1880 to 1893 the Loop in Chicago was the center of architectural development for the whole world. In a brief period of time the immense architectural possibilities in structural steel were explored. "Form follows function," which Louis Sullivan gleaned from Horatio Greenough and reiterated in his *Kindergarten Chats*, became the key to understanding the relationship between function and material, making possible — making even morally necessary — new architectural forms.

But while a Louis Sullivan was designing the office buildings, the warehouses and the factories which shaped modern architecture, the churches imitated the past. The now unfashionable sections of the same city are dotted with vast church buildings, vain monuments to middle-class ecclesiastical pride and reminders that the church failed to understand the religious and social meaning of their buildings and their time. For they designed their church buildings in terms of the past rather than the living present anticipating the future.

I understand it is one of the axioms of the architectural profession that architecture always tells the truth about the society in which it takes form. However much an age may try to disguise itself, its real nature is disclosed because architecture is the most social of all the arts. Architecture, therefore, is one of the most significant indices of the spiritual climate of an age. Among the best architects today one finds a concern for the social and religious significance of architecture that is not matched by the churches. These architects are concerned with the importance of good design in man's total life and particularly with the importance of good design for the church building and its allied arts. To these architects the restoration of spiritual health to present-day society involves the restoration to the church building of the symbolic and formative role which it once possessed in man's common life. No doubt many clergymen and churches would be surprised to learn that the best architects of our time, established ones and younger men launching their professional careers, are eager to design churches, and that many architectural students put their greatest effort and imaginative thought into church buildings. The best architectural talent is available to the churches. But Protestant churches for the most part have not faced as yet the fundamental task of freeing the architect from the fetters of style (whether it be Gothic, Renaissance, or modern) and giving the architect instead the ingredients for a sound exercise of his profession.

Church function and church form

The credo ascribed to Louis Sullivan, "Form follows function," points to the basic problem of good architecture for the Church. If this article were to have a text, it would be this: a church building which is effectively designed in terms of the function of the Church (and the particular congregation for which the building is erected) will have an appropriate form and thus the building may take on the nature of a symbol, saying to the world something of what the Church believes.

But before this can be achieved the Church must have a clearer understanding of its function, its vocation, in the world — in today's *and* tomorrow's world. In a sense architecture cannot reach its proper achievement until there has been a theological recovery within the Church of the meaning of the Church. Architecture is sometimes referred to as the queen of the arts and theology as the queen of sciences. They can never usurp each other's thrones, but unless their respective realms are in deep communication with each other, the one will thwart the other in the architecture and life of the Church. One of the important consequences of the ecumenical movement, represented institutionally in the World Council of Churches and in the National Council of Churches, is the growing awareness of the various traditions in the whole Church. and the rich meanings in the Church's heritage and present life which point to its fundamental vocation and function in the world.

On the other hand, one of the difficulties of church architecture in the past has been frequently that architectural form has followed too closely an inadequately conceived function. An architect can design a building, to be sure, for a church needing units to house its diverse activities. While the architect must have data on religious education requirements and space needs for the various groups in the church, the architect's task demands more than this. Fundamentally, he must know the Church's *raison d'être*. This understanding of the Church's purpose must be discovered by the minister and the congregation. The architect cannot be the theologian for the Church, just as the minister and the congregation cannot be the architect. In fact, more architects should say "no" to a church until the church is ready to say "yes" to its responsibility of rethinking its faith and life and work. A wise and spiritually discerning architect can thereby be of inestimable service to the Church. His insistence on the Church fulfilling its responsibility can be the catalyst in the Church's reassessment of itself and rediscovery of the source of its life.

Nikolas Pevsner, in a speech a few years ago on the proposed new Coventry Cathedral, said, "the function of the Church building is to convert visitors into worshippers." A building does not have the power of converting a visitor into a Christian worshipper, perhaps, but a building can hinder and distort the worship of the Church. Worship is central to the life of the Church. It is the Church's primary function and what the Church has always done before it has done anything else. Long before there were church schools and youth programs and community service, long before these and the multitude of activities of a contemporary parish church, the Church engaged in corporate worship. For worship is the heart of the Church's life and work. In fact, it has been asserted that the entire program of religious education is preparation of young and old for participation in the corporate act of worshipping God. Corporate worship sums up all the activities and the meaning of the Church.

One of the distinctions between the Judaeo-Christian tradition, between the Church and eastern religions, is the existence of a community, a fellowship into which men enter. While personal devotion and private worship are not denied, worship in the Christian community is a communal act. Therefore a church building must be designed not for the worship of the individual alone with the Alone, but for a corporate fellowship called to a purpose in the world.

The building should be shaped by worship, and not worship by architecture. But for some time Protestants have been erecting buildings designed to achieve a "mood" in which an individual might have a "worship experience" rather than a setting for the activity of the Church in showing its Lord in worship before the world.

However, we are on the threshold of new insights into worship as a result of the ecumenical movement. We are entering a period of rediscovery of the Church similar to other great periods in the history of Christianity. As in those times of renewal of life, the Church is reviving its historical memories, trying to find what has made the various denominations worship in different ways, and discover the unity which is higher and deeper than the differences. Architecture for the Church building, particularly the location of the altar, is a key to perceiving our differences.

"In the course of history, the Church has evolved three different types of altar, the mysterious, the dramatic, the ministerial. There is the altar of the eastern Christians, the mysterious altar hidden behind veils or the iconastasis; and frequently the Church in the west has tried to make the altar partially mysterious by the use of the chancel screen, the Lenten veil, the placing of the clergy and choir between the altar and the people. There is the dramatic altar, the altar of the baroque architects, of the Victorian ritualists, of numerous modern churches; an altar which by dramatic methods — ornament, the beauty of space, the manipulation of light and shadow — is made the showpiece of the church, and suggests to the worshipper the glory of the Sacrament. There is the ministerial altar, the holy table, a place of ministering, where our Lord perpetuates His ministry here on earth by the gift of heavenly food to the faithful gathered around it." (Addleshaw & Etchells, *The Architectural Setting of Anglican Worship*)

The mysterious altar is found without exception in Eastern Orthodox churches as well as in many of the Gothic buildings of Western Christianity. Eastern Orthodox churches continue to be constructed in such a way that the altar is hidden from the congregation. The dramatic altar is found in Baroque churches, whether they be Roman Catholic or Lutheran. And many contemporary Protestant church buildings are designed to make the altar spectacularly the object of attention in the Baroque manner. The ministerial altar is the Holy Table of the early Church and the Church of the first several centuries. In certain respects the Reformation was an attempt to restore the ministerial altar, the holy table.

The table and the pulpit

For example, as soon as the Reformation was established with some assurance of tenure, the reformed Church of England sought to accommodate its buildings to its new understanding of the Church. While practically no new church construction was undertaken until the last half of the 17th century, architectural changes were made in the existing buildings. The choir or chancel, which had been filled with stalls for monks or secular clergy, was cleared of its furniture and often the Table was moved forward or turned to extend lengthwise down the chancel. In the Book of Common Prayer order for Holy Communion at the point when the faithful were invited, "Ye that do truly and earnestly repent . . . draw near with faith," those who were to take communion came from the nave into the chancel and gathered about the Lord's Table to celebrate as a community the communion of the Lord's Supper.

In other expressions of the Reformation, the entire building became the sanctuary as the belief in the priesthood of all believers extended participation in the liturgy to the entire people. The first church built in Scotland after the Reformation, St. Cuthbert's of Burntisland in 1592, constituted an attempt to reckon architecturally with the implications of the Reformation. The church was designed in the shape of a Greek cross, and the great pulpit was thrust from one of the arms of the cross into the heart of the congregation, and placed in front of it was a large Table, around which a host of persons might sit. Pulpit and Table, in classic Protestantism, are theologically and liturgically united, and early Protestantism was chiefly concerned that architecture reflect this basic conviction.

This tradition of pulpit and Table closely related continued for some time. In fact, there was a remarkable unity of architectural form in 18th-century colonial America. It arose out of a common understanding of the nature of the Church and its function. Thus one found Congregational churches in New England, Dutch Reformed churches in New York, Presbyterian churches in New Jersey, Lutheran churches in Pennsylvania, and Episcopal churches in Virginia, all having a large pulpit in the center and a Table of goodly proportions before it, emphasizing the centrality of the Word and the unity of the Word in its two forms of Scripture and Lord's Supper.

The architectural tradition of a meeting house for Protestant churches disappeared nearly a century ago. The great pulpit, designed in scale with the interior, shrank in the 19th century to a lectern, badly out of scale with the building, and placed on a platform or rostrum. The organ and choir, which in the meeting house were in the rear gallery, were moved to the dominating position in back of the generally tiny Table and spindly lectern. Out of this emerged the so-called Akron plan. Disastrous as it was architecturally, this much-derided pattern of church building was well designed for the church of its day. It was well planned for hearing a speaker and choir or quartet, for accommodating the extra crowds which would come to hear a striking address, and for the growing emphasis on religious instruction for young and old in the church rather than the home. The inadequacy of this kind of building for Protestantism, so apparent to us now, derived from the diminishing understanding of the full spiritual dimensions of the Church. It stands as an architectural reminder that before it builds the Church must think profoundly about itself and see its function in terms of the Bible, tradition, and the present world.

The emptiness of vacuity

Even so the Akron plan was designed for a church still nourished by evangelical roots. As these roots dried, however, there was confusion about the building and concern over its barrenness. With the increasing decay of preaching the room for worship became empty, not in Professor Tillich's conception of "holy emptiness," but the emptiness of vacuity. Protestant churches sought to fill the emptiness by copying church traditions other than their own and by introducing pictures, crosses. Rather than looking to their own past they found an ideal in the Episcopal Church, in its worship, in its music, and above all in its architecture, generally Gothic in character with an altar, choir stalls, and the Bible no longer on the pulpit but on a lectern on the opposite side of the chancel. During recent decades when Presbyterian, Congregational, Methodist, and Baptist churches were appropriating architectural arrangements from them, Episcopalians were not yet conscious of how recent and unjustified was their introduction of medieval altars and monastic choir arrangements into their parish churches.

Thus the churches in America today find themselves confronted with liturgical and theological anachronisms. They are attempting to worship in buildings that imply beliefs they do not hold and patterns of worship they do not practice. Fortunately, immense resources of new thinking about these matters are available from the leaders of the Church. The most recent Biblical, theological, and liturgical works are in remarkable agreement. The Church, they say, is a family, a people, a community, called into being to serve a purpose. And the nature of its life, its worship, its vocation and its function in the world demands altogether new approaches to worship and architecture. There is recognition of the uniqueness of each denominational tradition and at the same time a growing understanding of the basic unity of the Church.

The free-standing altar

It is one of the ironies of history that the liturgical movement in the Roman Catholic Church is seeking to recover the ministerial altar at a time when Protestants have been approaching the architectural setting for worship in ways that the fathers of the Reformation rejected. In the Roman Catholic Church, the liturgical movement, for instance, has rejected the medieval altar in favor of a free-standing altar, sometimes even resembling a table. Several new churches designed with the altar in the center imply that the same currents are at work as are found in the ecumenical movement. The central position of the altar suggests that the Church is a family gathered for its Holy Meal. Such a central plan, which many Roman Catholic churches are adopting, is not easily arranged for Protestants because for them the liturgical orientation is not to an altar alone but to an altar (Table) *and* a pulpit and a font or baptistry.

The architectural anachronisms of many Protestant church buildings will become even more apparent in the future as the confluence of Biblical, theological, and liturgical studies results in re-examination and renewal of worship. It has already commenced at the level of the World Council of Churches and in theological seminaries. When it becomes fully apparent, much of the church building of the last few decades will be seen to be imitative, eclectic, and impressionistic.

Fortunately, there are several striking examples in the United States of serious reflection and fresh thinking by a local congregation engaged in an informed dialogue with the architect. Pietro Belluschi's design for the Presbyterian Church in Cottage Grove, Oregon, shows what can happen as a result of cooperation between minister, congregation, and architect. But this building is not to be imitated. The thorough exploration in the congregation of what it means to be a Church, what it means to belong to a particular tradition of the whole Church, and what it means for the Church to try to speak simply but directly in terms of our day — it is this exploration and reflection which should be emulated by all congregations preparing to erect a new house of worship. The building program then becomes not an expression of the Church's self-concern but the occasion of spiritual renewal.

A church building not only houses the public worship and related life of a religious community. It becomes a symbol to the secular community of what the Church is and what it believes. If architecture arises out of the faith and common life of the Church it can accentuate the religious apprehensions of the worshippers, reinforce the beliefs and memories which the Church shares. Manifestly, architecture cannot create faith, but it can express aspects of the faith which is given. A church building can express the transcendence and the immanence of God; it can suggest that the Church escapes from the world or that the Church lives in but not of the world; it can imply that the Church can speak only to those within it or that the Church speaks to the world it confronts.

The Judaeo-Christian tradition affirms that God is both transcendent and immanent. He is beyond space and time and cannot be confined to a particular place or moment, culture or age. On the other hand, God is present in the living Church, acting in the events of history and in our common life. In the Incarnation, the Church asserts, God entered our world at a particular place and time.

Space is the symbol of God

I believe that the transcendence and immanence of God can be expressed in church architecture today perhaps better than ever before. The concern of contemporary architects with space and the relationship and inter-penetration of interior and exterior space can be highly significant. Professor Tillich asserts that space is our most valid symbol of God. The God who cannot be contained or "spatialized" is represented by definition of space which covers man in his finitude. With today's building materials and techniques it is possible to achieve architectural space of symbolic power. I believe that the Church building of our day can best express God's transcendence of space and time as it also expresses the immanence of God in employing the space and time possibilities of modern architecture.

The plea, "I want a church building to look like a church," is not to be dismissed. A church building should be a symbol of the Church. This is the problem faced by the Christian movement since its inception. How can the Christian message be expressed afresh in each new age, in cultures other than our own? Yet the Christian faith which derives from the Incarnation must become incarnate in each person, in each generation. As the Christian faith becomes manifest in flesh and blood, so it must become manifest in stone, concrete, glass, and steel.

Architecture for the Church, for this reason, becomes the highest challenge which confronts an architect. Equipped with a congregation's knowledge of itself, its history, and its present life, the architect must design a building that suggests the Church is a people with a history, whose source of life is beyond history, and whose work is in the present — the now that will be the history of tomorrow — and whose destiny is beyond history and this life.

The tent as a prototype

Daniel Jenkins, a Congregational pastor and theologian, has offered the interesting thought that the tent is the prototype of the ideal building for the Church. In connection with its Hebrew antecedents it suggests a building for a people on the march, the Church ready to move on to new frontiers. Paul Schweikher's design for a Methodist church, which is reminiscent of a circular tent, represents an interesting fusion of the tent motif, American religious history, and present-day design. The new circular chapel at M.I.T. is also an appropriation of an ancient religious form, the circle. Rudolf Schwarz has explored the symbolism of the different forms of the church building. His doubt of the religious validity of the circle in terms of the Christian faith suggests that no form in itself will answer the problem of church design. The forms of architecture arise at the intersection of God's action toward man and man's response to God in community with his fellows. Architectural symbolism must arise from the Church's life and a building appropriate to it, rather than by imposing a "universal" symbolic form on architecture.

Do our church buildings imply that the Church seeks to escape from the world or that the Church lives in but not of the world? Do the buildings suggest the Church has a message for the world or only for itself? Several churches built during the last few years illustrate the problem that every Church and architect must confront. In St. Clement's at Alexandria, Virginia, a church was designed with an altar in the center and the congregation on opposite sides, the choir over the entrance supposedly uniting the two parts of the congregation. This building represents a serious attempt to recognize the Church as a family gathered about its Holy Table. But there are no windows. Overhead pinpoints of light provide illumination in what might be a catacomb of darkness. Economy of construction prompted the use of windowless exterior walls, but the symbolism becomes a matter of importance. In obedience to its faith, can a Church shut out all evidence of the world of nature? It has been suggested that this particular building points to a truth about the Church in our world. Despite its present outward success, this argument states, the Church is forced to withdraw within itself, cutting itself off from the world in order to renew its life and strength, that at the right time it may go forth and transform the world.

In contrast, St. Stephen's Church in Columbus, Ohio, makes interesting use of a glass wall which relates the church to the world. Numerous churches have been built in which the worshippers look across the "altar" through clear glass windows into a forest or a mountain view. In such churches the ultimate focus is the world of nature. St. Stephen's resisted both the temptation to nature worship on the one hand and complete withdrawal from the world on the other. Through windows at one side a garden court may be seen, but worship is oriented to a Holy Table above which is suspended a cross. The glass wall is at the entrance to the church building. While the church is worshipping in a building, the world may catch a glimpse of the mystery which the Church declares in its worship to the world. The congregation on leaving the building is conscious of the world to which the Church must witness. This building was designed for the function of the Church in the modern world. But it symbolizes a community which exists in the world, serves the community in which it lives in the name of a higher community from which it derives its life, and points to our ultimate fulfillment in that higher community.

A proper procedure

1. Before an architect is selected the church should engage in a thorough study of itself. Study your denominational heritage, its beliefs about the Church, its tradition of worship, its attitude toward the arts, its overall understanding of its function in the world and in the community. Review this study in the light of the Bible. One of America's outstanding laymen, an industrialist who wants good architecture for the church, suggests that a congregation study the New Testament before it decides to build. In this way tradition and the Church's present life will be brought together under the creative judgment of God's disclosure.

2. Because the minister has had theological seminary training it should not be assumed that he does not need personally to engage in even more thorough study. Having been a Dean of Students and Director of Studies in a theological seminary for several years, I know how the seminaries have failed to give adequate training in these matters. Let the minister be the first to submit himself to a discipline of study.

3. The church should review its program in the light of the fresh insights of these studies. Questions such as these might be asked: should the church building be designed in terms of the existing pattern of the Church's life, or should the building anticipate the changes in worship, religious education, and fellowship which a thorough study of the Church may suggest are God's will.

4. Look, then, for the best architect you can find. Some of the great buildings for the Church have been designed by comparatively young architects of outstanding ability or by architects who have never before designed a church building. When the church is ready to retain an architect, several architects may be interviewed. Not the architect who agrees most readily with what predilections may remain within a church after a thorough study, but the architect who challenges the church to further thinking, may well be the architect who will serve the larger purpose of the Church. If the local church fulfills its responsibility of developing a clear conception of itself, its nature and its function, the truly imaginative architect will draw upon all his talents. The result may be a building for which future generations will rise up and call you blessed!

5. The *Handbook of Architectural Practice*, published by the American Institute of Architects, 1741 New York Ave., N.W., Washington, D. C., will be of great help to the Building Committee. Several shorter documents can be obtained in quantity for a few cents each and will insure understanding on the part of the local church of its relationship to the architect. These are: A.I.A. Document #225, *Principles of Professional Practice;* A.I.A. Document #300, The *Selection of an Architect;* and A.I.A. Document #177, *Details of Service to be Rendered and Schedule of Proper Charges for Services.*

6. After you have selected an architect, proceed to selection of a site. The architect's advice can save a local church from grievous errors. There may be circumstances which necessitate procuring a site before an architect is retained. In all events it is assumed that a local church works in cooperation with its appropriate denominational agencies and with the council of churches in planning and comity.

7. If the church's study suggests that art properly may be used in the church building, make adequate provision to use the work of living artists rather than mass-produced liturgical arts. Make certain that the architect's plans include all the liturgical items appropriate to your church's way of worship. Many otherwise fine buildings have been disfigured by the intrusion of crosses, candlesticks, communion vessels, fabrics, and other items that violate the integrity of the architect's work. The director of the nearest art museum can put the church and architect in touch with competent artists. As with architects, the best artists may not be the ones who aggressively seek a commission from the church. The best artists of our day, however, will respond with enthusiasm to an invitation to do work for the Church. Let us use them.

8. While Protestantism has been negligent in the visual arts, it has employed and often fostered the musical arts. The budget for a church building should include provision for a pipe organ. A church building is not complete for worship without one. Again the church should turn for competent advice, for instance, to the head of the organ department in a leading college or university.

* K. T. I. SYNAGOGUE, PORT CHESTER, N. Y.

Philip Johnson, Architect
Marcello Mezzullo, Contractor
Eipel Engineering, Structural Engineers
Charles Middeleer, Landscape Architect
Ibram Lassaw, Sculpture
Richard Kelly, Lighting Consultant
John Johansen, Stained Glass Consultant

* *Kneses Tifereth Israel*

The intellectual appeal of clear, structural articulation and the sensual delights inherent in precise craftsmanship are real, though limited, satisfactions. In a time which often seems to have restricted its reverence to these particulars it is especially rewarding to find a building which provides in addition some positive and fruitful answers to problems of approach and scale and color and light. In this synagogue a full range of human and structural requirements has been accepted and organized into an instructive and inspirational example.

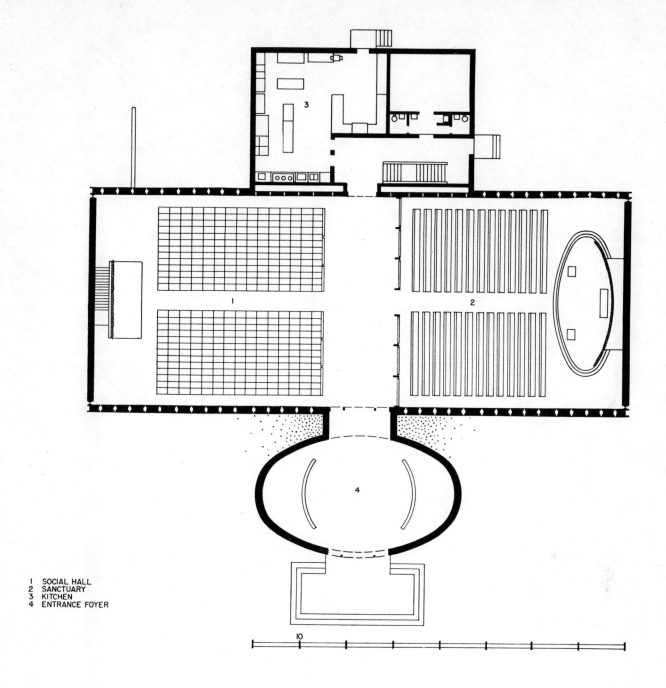

1 SOCIAL HALL
2 SANCTUARY
3 KITCHEN
4 ENTRANCE FOYER

10

FROM THE APPROACH along Port Chester's King Street, the building is suddenly seen sitting high and very white against the trees. It is bigger than its pictures have suggested and this feeling is enhanced by the way in which the entrance drive, moving parallel to the south face of the building and then half-circling back to the doors, reveals progressively that essential relationship of the small oval entrance pavilion to the large rectilinear hall which has such powerful consequences in terms of scale.

This is a monumental building and its patterns and penetrations as well as its profiles are all arranged to make it so. The panels are just over the height of a man and they, rather than the openings, afford the kind of human dimensional identification necessary to the sense of bigness which is achieved when they are multiplied into five ascending tiers.

From the first this building is revealed as an accomplished exercise in scale and the conviction grows as one moves from out under the sky through the large dark doors into the small compressive ellipse of the vestibule, and from there on into the expansive — almost explosive — space of a hall which seems higher than its thirty-seven feet. And light, which contributes in so many ways to scale, has

been manipulated equally well. The organization is the classic sequence of light to dark to light again in which the transition from outside to inside is prevented from robbing the windows of either dimension or brilliance. White — again inside — is a compelling impression but here it is subtly slashed from floor to ceiling and end to end with the Joseph's coat palette of the stained glass light slits. The colors have great clarity. Each is used separately in a single slit and there are just enough clear panels to fortify the lighter colors and to contrast the full richness of the dark reds and blues. The floor is a white-streaked, light gray asphalt tile; the straight

rows of three hundred theater seats in the sanctuary are upholstered in a light silver gray which picks up just a little of the blues and reds from the glass. The bema is covered in gold colored carpeting and the screen behind it is clad in a metallic white acoustic cloth.

Across the middle, dividing the sanctuary and the social areas, are the parallel lines of eight-foot partitions which, framed in aluminum and steel braced, are bolted to the floor for easy removal on the High Holidays when over 1000 must be accommodated. Above all sail seven gently curving suspended vaults of plaster, giving a particular sense of containment to this space through their spe-

cial ability to modulate the daylight and serving themselves as both light sources and baffles. In each rib are the direct downlights — six dark piercings when unlit, and only partially concealed behind the sail's incurving sides are the dimmer-controlled lights which, directed toward the sidewalls, let the building glow at night like the "box of jewels" that had been promised even in its preliminary planning.

Perhaps only in the piercing of the plaster canopies does one find anything out of harmony in this inspirational space and even here it is difficult to find fault. The downlights and spotlights which undeniably re-move some of the free-floating quality of the ceiling are nevertheless essential to the equally important control of illumination.

Here the architect has chosen the more difficult and more commendable path. He has been willing to admit into a kind of formal purity — even at the risk of its partial dilution — the means of a larger satisfaction. This may well be the most significant story of this rewarding building. To a structural system of great precision and beautiful proportions has been added a concern for light, and color, and the way people use and experience buildings: with *all* their senses *and* their intellects.

William Wollin Studio

ST. JOSEPH'S CHURCH, FT. ATKINSON, WIS.

**John J. Flad and Associates,
 Architects**
T. S. Willis, General Contractor

At eighty-eight cents a cubic foot and on a congested corner site these architects have been able to create for a traditional liturgy and a conventional program of requirements a building of many positive architectural achievements. Most dramatic of these is the enormous stained-glass mural which dominates the entrance face and which — particularly at night — provides a rich tapestry of light as the focus of an ensemble which inevitably reveals the harsh demands of a rigidly restricted budget, but achieves distinction nevertheless.

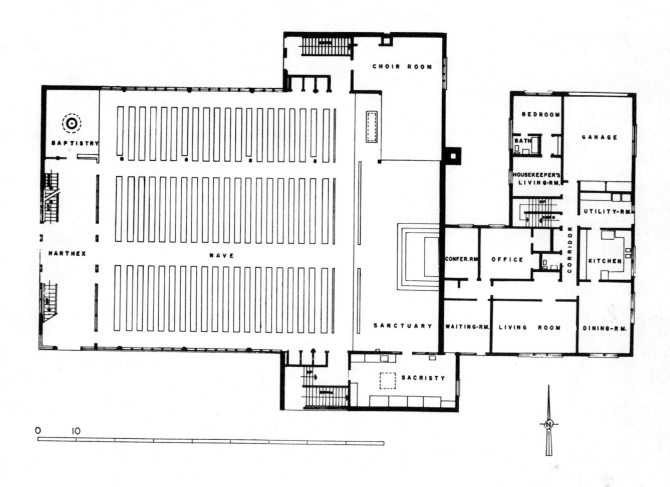

CHOIR ROOM

BAPTISTRY

NARTHEX

NAVE

BEDROOM

BATH

GARAGE

HOUSEKEEPER'S LIVING-RM.

UTILITY-RM.

CONFER.RM OFFICE CORRIDOR KITCHEN

SANCTUARY WAITING-RM. LIVING ROOM DINING-RM.

SACRISTY

0 10

N

William Wollin Studio

NAVE, BALCONY, AND CHOIR can seat just over 700 on this site crowded with an existing two-story school and with the necessity of providing with the church a fairly elaborate rectory facility. Circulation between these elements was a primary problem and has been handled well along with the principal approach which is by means of an offset terrace.

Immediately off the narthex is a completely enclosed baptistery lighted through the low roof which, continuing over the side aisle, gives emphasis to the higher nave and acts as visual transition between church and school.

The principal material is a buff-range brick exposed throughout the interior and which —

both inside and out — serves as a neutral background for the two principal color foci. Of these the great window tells its story in blues and reds with minor accents. It was designed by Burckhard and executed by the Esser Studio of Milwaukee, as was the altar mural, which was designed by Erhard Stoettner in Venetian glass tile mosaic.

All major materials are in their natural colors. Pews and trim are in birch, and the rectory uses redwood siding.

A large parish hall with adjacent lounge, meeting rooms, and kitchen occupies the entire basement level. Total cost of building was $295,000.

Dearborn-Massar

EMMANUEL PRESBYTERIAN CHURCH, SPOKANE

McClure & Adkinson,
   Architects
Lyle C. Campbell,
   Structural Engineer
Kendall Wood & Associates,
   Mechanical Engineers
Joseph Doyle,
   Electrical Engineer

Fine scale, the skillful use of a limited site, and a very positive expression of an invitation to withdrawal are the qualities which particularly recommended publication of this church. Of these the latter is almost unique today. Here a welcoming reach is made to the community through the covered entrance walk alongside the pleasantly placed tree and yet it is everywhere manifest that the community is being welcomed to withdraw in worship. Welcome and withdrawal are a difficult duality and in a small building are seldom achieved simultaneously.

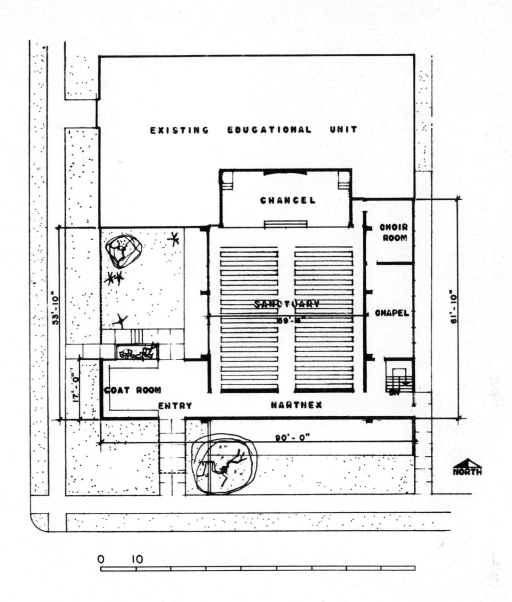

EXISTING EDUCATIONAL UNIT

CHANCEL

CHOIR ROOM

SANCTUARY
59'-8"

CHAPEL

53'-10"

61'-10"

17'-0"

COAT ROOM

ENTRY

NARTHEX

90'-0"

NORTH

0   10

NO WINDOWS FACE THE STREET and once inside the natural light sources are arranged to enhance that sense of removal which is both theologically and sensuously effective. The hollowed recession of the first bay over the brick-screened, sky-lighted narthex contributes strongly to the visual pull and to the plastic participation of interior and exterior spaces. This recessed wall is clad in acid-treated copper and while for some there may be an overabundance of materials certainly no one would wish to delete this one which forms such a rich background for the white enamelled cross and which extends downward to form the interior narthex wall.

The program asked the architects for a sanctuary for 400, sympathetic to the already existing educational wing and within a hemmed in site. The side location of entry and coat area, which was in direct response to the property limitation, produces the useful court and partially contributes to the sense of retreat. Relationship of new and existing basement levels required the forward light well. Principal framing elements are the glue laminated arches. Exterior surfaces are brick, painted plaster and copper; interior repeats these plus walnut and asbestos cement panels, acoustic, ceramic and asphalt tile. All sanctuary furnishings were designed by the architects.

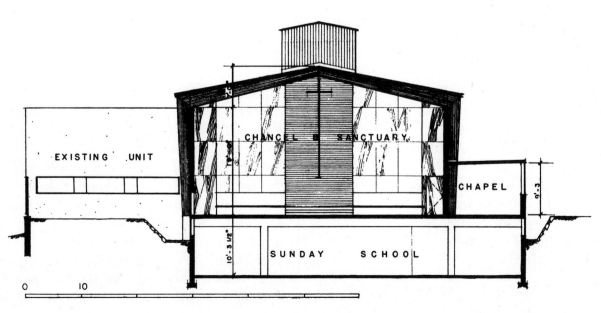

EXISTING UNIT

CHANCEL & SANCTUARY

CHAPEL

SUNDAY SCHOOL

0   10

LATERAL SECTION

SCALE: 1/8" = 1'-0"

Hedrich-Blessing

TEMPLE BETH EL, GARY, IND.

Percival Goodman, Architect
Faioli, Blum & Yesselman,
  Structural Engineers
William Dusenbury, Mechanical
  Engineer
Gerometta Construction Co.,
  General Contractors
Seymour Lipton, Sculptor
Hans Moller, Designer of
  ark curtain

Historically the synagogue in the west has been relatively free of strong traditions in architectural form which have made modern design for Christian worship a most exacting exercise. The architect of talent has been able generally to express the relationship of the Jewish Community to the general community and nowhere has this been done more clearly than in this synagogue which has been fashioned in steel against the background of a steelworking city. Especially clear is the arrangement for the three part function of worship, study and social gathering,

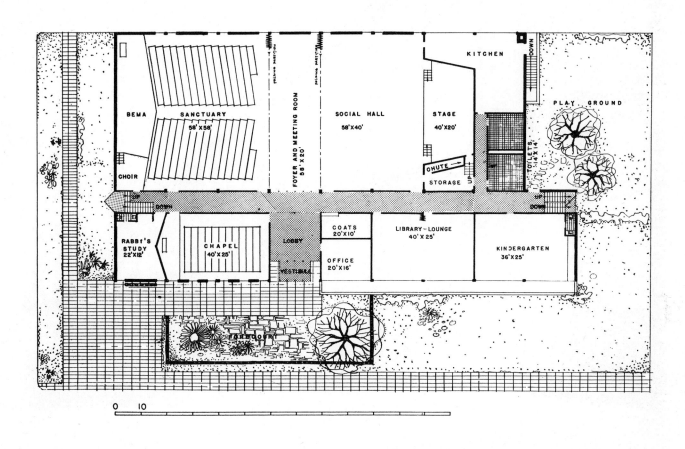

BEMA

SANCTUARY
58' X 58'

CHOIR

FOYER AND MEETING ROOM
58' X 20'

SOCIAL HALL
58' X 40'

STAGE
40' X 20'

KITCHEN

DOWN

CHUTE

STORAGE

TOILETS
14' X 14'

PLAY GROUND

RABBI'S
STUDY
22' X 12'

CHAPEL
40' X 25'

LOBBY

VESTIBULE

COATS
20' X 10'

OFFICE
20' X 16'

LIBRARY - LOUNGE
40' X 25'

KINDERGARTEN
36' X 25'

DOWN

UP   DOWN

0   10

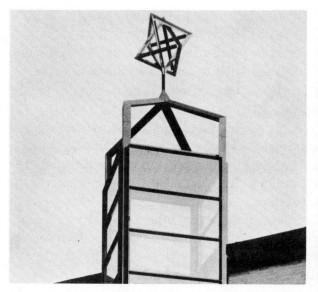

which so characterizes the good synagogue today. In an orderly, economical, and direct architectural expression perhaps only the triangular stair tower projection will be questioned — and that for its proportion rather than intention.

IN THE OTHERWISE rectangular framework of exposed standard steel sections the architect has placed panels of brick, granite or glass. A projecting canopy covers the entrance from the gathering place within the walled forecourt. To the left the welded metal sculpture in the menorah theme is by Seymour Lipton. Directly ahead of the lobby is a central lounge whose partitions fold away on either side to open up the 22 ft high sanctuary and social

hall whose combined seating capacity is 1000. The ark which dominates the sanctuary is framed in black and white veined marble and is covered with a curtain in brilliant color designed by Hans Moller. The menorah and the eternal light over the ark are by Lipton.

A chapel for small weddings and services, a multi-use library, a well equipped kindergarten and administrative offices complete the main floor. Above are nine classrooms and the custodian's apartment and in the basement are several meeting rooms and a large playroom. All adjunct faculties are designed for the maximum flexibility demanded by the heavy and varied use of the building.

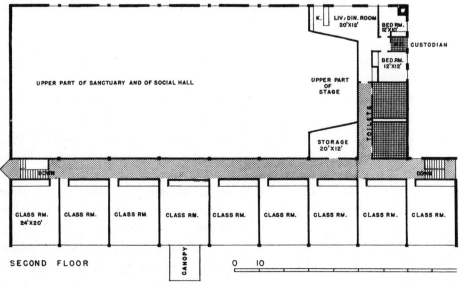

UPPER PART OF SANCTUARY AND OF SOCIAL HALL

K. | LIV.-DIN. ROOM 20'X12'

BED RM. 12'X10'

CUSTODIAN

BED.RM. 12'X12'

UPPER PART OF STAGE

STORAGE 20'X12'

CLASS RM. 24'X20' | CLASS RM. | CLASS RM. | CLASS RM. | CLASS RM. | CLASS RM. | CLASS RM. | CLASS RM. | CLASS RM.

SECOND FLOOR

CANOPY

0   10

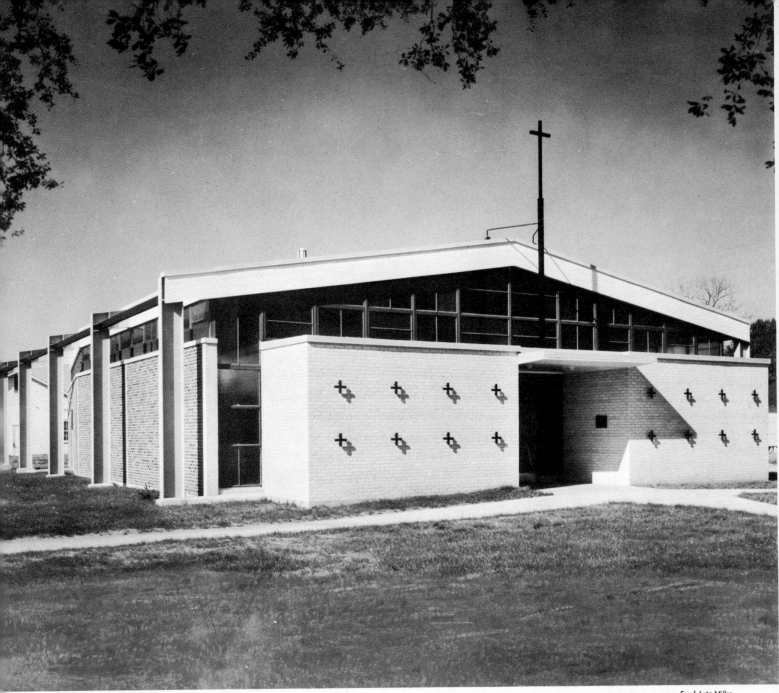

IMMACULATE CONCEPTION CHAPEL, JENNINGS, LA.

Burk, Lebreton & Lamantia,
   Architects
Bartley & Binnings, General
   Contractors

On a budget of $65,000 which rigidly restricted design to the manipulation of the shape and color of a few simple materials the architects have created for this outlying area of a Louisiana parish a chapel of real distinction. The building is carefully made and achieves its success through this as well as through an expansive quality of the interior space which is generated by the well arranged natural light sources and the flat-bowing of the non-loaded brick side walls.

The desirable sense of withdrawal has been almost fully attained without sacrifice of the sense

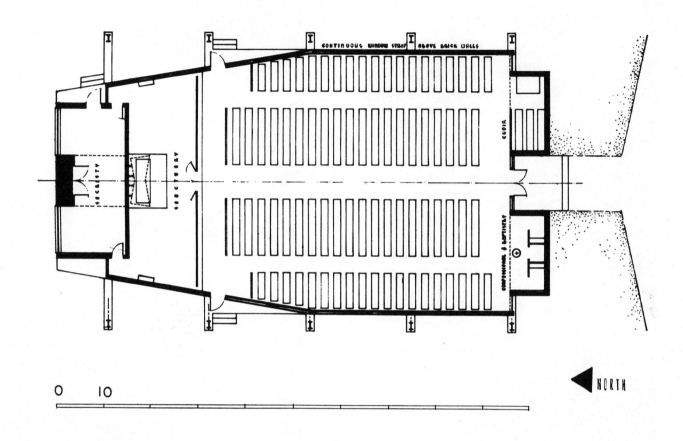

CONTINUOUS WINDOW STRIP ABOVE BRICK WALLS

CHOIR

CONFESSIONAL & BAPTISTRY

SACRISTY

RECTORY

0   10

▲ NORTH

of welcome which is afforded, in part, by the transitional spaces under the eaves and behind the rank of supports. The penetration of these 10-in. hollow core brick walls with exit doors seems an unhappy necessity in an otherwise splendid geometry of concrete stabilization posts, brick infilling, and steel sash patterns.

THESE LATTER ARE GLAZED in delicate tints of marine antique glass. Although the building is not constantly open regular services are offered for 400 people. The rigid steel frame carries a steel deck with built-up composition roof. The exposed deck constitutes the ceiling finish except over the chancel bay where an acoustical ceiling is hung to conceal electrical work, reduce noise, and provide an accent over the altar as well.

The floor is of concrete on earth fill with an added surface that was hardened, colored and waxed.

The wall separating sanctuary and sacristy, the canopy over the altar, and confessionals are of white oak plywood. The custom built furniture includes oak pews, a communion rail in oak and steel, a marble altar with iron candlesticks. The crucifix is of wood with a terra cotta corpus. Tabernacle is a stock steel box painted and suspended by bronze bars. All furnishings are included in the total cost as stated.

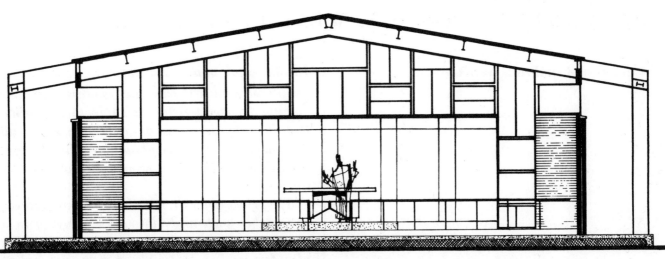

0   10

6541

ST. MARTHA'S MISSION, WEST COVINA, CAL.

Carleton Winslow, Architect

In the final analysis instructive examples of architecture must possess and express either one dominant characteristic which is so appealing that it integrates — or at least overrides — all other aspects, or some combination of less forceful appeals which have been brought to unmistakable unity.

The proposal for St. Martha's Mission Church approaches such unity through employing in a simple constructional system a direct expression of a few modern materials, a rich color palette and a happy relationship of building to site.

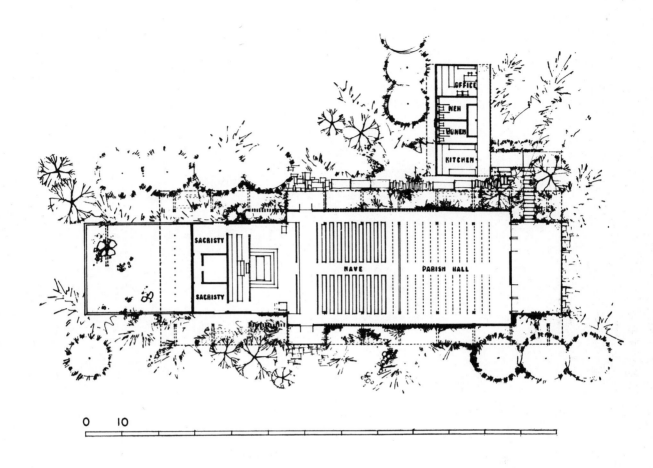

SACRISTY

NAVE   PARISH HALL

SACRISTY

OFFICE

NEH

UNEH

KITCHEN

0   10

Beyond the question of the appropriateness of its Oriental character for an Episcopal parish in a Los Angeles suburb there is a quality here which recommends the attention of all who must build to limited budgets as well as to those more fortunately funded.

WHEN COMPLETED THIS BUILDING will stand in a grove of trees with a tall, white wooden cross rising from the side of a pool which has been arranged to reflect the end wall of the sanctuary. The wall, which is blue, will be lightly screened by a grid of wires supporting small gold crosses.

The building frame consists of laminated beams carried on square wood posts well be-yond the side walls to keep out the direct sun-light. The broad overhangs are thus a response to a natural force in the region but provide as well — along with the range of supports which stand free of the building sides — an inviting cushion of space between the inside and the outside.

The side walls are to be entirely of burnt orange glass. Other colors are blue green, gray and royal blue.

Designed to seat 550, one end of the 150-ft. building can be closed off with sliding walls to function as a parish hall. The use of existing trees and the scaling of the building to them is unusual and rewarding.

SEVENTY THOUSAND CHURCHES IN TEN YEARS

By George Cline Smith, Assistant Vice President and Economist, F. W. Dodge Corporation

THE CURRENT UPSURGE of interest in religion is actually part of a long-term trend which has been expressed in rising membership of churches, both absolutely and in proportion to the population, through several decades. Other manifestations of this growing emphasis on church-going, which were noted in an article ("More Church Building Is Required to Keep Pace with Membership Growth") in the Dec. 1954 issue of ARCHITECTURAL RECORD include a sharp increase in the number of members per church structure, indicating some tendency toward overcrowding, and a rise in church spending and building which seems to offer considerable room for further expansion to meet the demand of a growing, moving and more church-minded population.

The spiritual significance of this trend should be obvious. There is, as well, an economic side to the story of particular interest to architects and engineers.

The economic aspect of the situation boils down simply to this: it is reasonable to expect that in the coming ten years, some 70,000 churches and synagogues will be constructed or substantially altered at a total cost of nearly six billion dollars. In addition, there will be about 12,500 projects involving parish houses, Sunday schools and related buildings costing one and a quarter billion dollars. (Note: these estimates do not include parochial schools, which are classified as educational rather than religious buildings.)

This is considered to be a conservative estimate, in the light of past and present trends. It does make two important assumptions: first, that there will be no severe recession or depression during the period; and second, that there will be no major war. The estimate contemplates an average level of activity over the ten-year period somewhat below that of 1954 and considerably below that attained in early 1955. It is entirely possible, therefore, that the estimate may be on the low side, in view of our rapid population growth and movement, current prosperity and the increasing emphasis on church-going.

It has been estimated that somewhere in the neighborhood of 5000 architectural firms work regularly or occasionally in the church field. During the next decade, therefore, the average firm may expect to have about 14 church projects at about $85,000 per job, and two or three other religious buildings at about $100,000 each. This adds up to nearly a million and a half dollars' worth of work for the average firm in the church field, during the ten-year period.

These figures are based on contract awards reported by F. W. Dodge Corporation in the 37 eastern states, with an adjustment to take care of the estimated volume of building in the remaining 11 states. The average cost per job is calculated from 1954 reports, and the estimate assumes that there will be no substantial change in the value of the dollar.

Current activity in church construction is running at the highest rate in history. Contract awards for religious buildings in the 37 eastern states during the first three months of 1955 totalled $128 million. That's an increase of 60 per cent above the previous first-quarter record set in 1951, and 61 per cent above the first quarter of 1954.

The religious category in the first quarter of 1955 accounted for about 7 per cent of all non-residential building awards. This represents an enormous growth, not only in dollars but in share of the market, during the postwar period. In the corresponding quarter of 1946, the first postwar year, religious buildings totalled only $17 million, and represented just 2 per cent of non-residential building.

The outlook for church building is bright. This is all to the good, because, in the words of Sir Thomas Browne, "They build not castles in the air who would build churches on earth; and though they leave no such structures here, may lay good foundations in Heaven."

WOULD YOU BUILD
ANOTHER CONTEMPORARY CHURCH?

You ask "Would you do it again?" My answer is that it *is* being done again — in my present parish — and that if the Lord sees fit to place me in other parishes where church plants are to be built, it would be done again and again. I can't help asking when I look at some new churches whether we are living in our own day or are kidding ourselves that we live in some past age. I believe that we should have the courage to be unashamed of our own expression of devotion to God.

If you are going to build a church of contemporary design, there are some things that you shouldn't overlook. The first of these is yourself. Are you convinced that beauty can be achieved from simple basic things like light, space, color, texture? Or do you still believe that it takes a pompous monument to make beauty? As the leader of your congregation, you first of all must be sure of the answer to these questions. Visit some churches of contemporary design; it will be worth all it may cost you. Don't just look at them; stay in them for several hours until you absorb the devotional atmosphere that makes them churches. Read a few good books on contemporary architecture, too. Convince yourself thoroughly that you want a contemporary design for your new church.

The second step is to condition your congregation. Many of them have never thought in terms of a church designed differently from that which their grandfathers built. Often people are unimaginative, and lazy, and hesitate to take a step forward even when they suspect it might be good for them. They need to be taught how to appreciate the contemporary. In talking with them, I would forget the suggestion that a contemporary design will cost less than a copy of a past style. You will do better to lead them into accepting the idea that they should erect a building which is an expression of their own devotion, not their fathers' or grandfathers'. This means a lot of work for you.

The third step is the selection of a committee, often called a "building committee." The building committee doesn't have to be large — three is a good number; its members should be strong and aggressive leaders who are also unbiased and fair-minded. The building committee does not need to know anything of construction if it is to function as I feel it should, as a means by which the architect and the congregation can conveniently communicate with each other. In fact, if the members know something about construction they are likely to burden the architect with ideas and, while some of these may be good, most of them will cause misunderstanding and confusion.

Selecting the architect requires utmost care. There are architects and architects and choosing between them is not easy. There are some — I sometimes think there are too few of them — who are truly creative. In interviewing architects, pay particular attention to whether a man understands such things as devotional quality and whether he indicates such an understanding without your prodding him. He should firmly believe that this devotional quality will emerge from space, light, color, texture; the right one will quickly and definitely disagree with you if you suggest otherwise. I particularly appreciated it when Mr. Belluschi in Portland informed us that if he could not create the devotional atmosphere which we wanted, he did not want to design the church.

Once you have determined the space requirements and budget, give the architect this information and ask him to go ahead. Let him use his imagination without hindrance — that is what you engage him for and that is what you pay him for. And, on the subject of fees, pay him the going rate so he can do a good job for you. When he presents the plot plan, accept it *in toto* or reject it *in toto*. The same holds for the final plan. If there are changes to be made — and there will be some — let the architect make them. In the measure that you or your committee or the congregation change the design it will be spoiled.

I'm no authority; but you can see from this that you have a very important and a very big job to do. There are still too few pastors with the courage and the faith to let their new buildings express a faith that is of today. But I can assure you that, if you do, you will be amply rewarded once the job is done.

Alwin L. Rubin, Pastor

The pastor of Trinity Lutheran, who was pastor in Portland, Ore., when Pietro Belluschi was selected as architect for Zion Lutheran Church in that city, answers the question of a fellow pastor

Concrete panels cast "in situ" by Bernard Frazier. They are forty feet high and were done for Temple Israel, Tulsa, Oklahoma. Percival Goodman, architect

WORSHIP AND THE ARTS

By Otto Spaeth

Mr. Spaeth is a founder and past president of the Liturgical Arts Society; a member of the American Federation of Arts: and a private collector

THE SIX RELIGIOUS BUILDINGS shown in this section, "Worship and the Arts," are compelling examples of what may be expected from a fruitful encounter between eternity and the moment. It was that encounter that raised the great churches of our European past and it is heartening to see it taking place again.

A continuity of essentials thus exists in ecclesiastical architecture of the first rank, and if surfaces change — sometimes apparently beyond recognition — it takes but a moment's thought on two of these essentials, "eternity" and "the moment," to see why this must be.

The moment changes, of course, or it would not be the moment. But the changes evident in the moment that inspired the best of these churches and temples are more profound than the availability of new materials for building, and new architectural concepts for handling those materials. The moment includes the whole present society in which the church is situated, the position of the church in that society, the intellectual texture of the congregation, the many and intricate relationships between the congregation and the society.

To illustrate: a thirteenth century cathedral dominates the thirteenth century cathedral-town partly because the thirteenth century Church did indeed dominate the society of that day. Dr. Blanchard aside, does anyone seriously pretend that any Church dominates contemporary American society?

"Eternity" changes, too. This blatant contradiction in terms is explained by the simple fact that in our vital encounter — certainly insofar as it takes place in ecclesiastical architecture — we are not really dealing with eternity, but, of necessity, with our own understanding of eternity. This is not theological relativism, but a simple recognition of the humility and truth in St. Paul's "through a glass darkly." From time to time the vision clears; from time to time the glass darkens. But at any time, we are stuck with the glass. Only through it can we glimpse the eternity which is to shape our lives and our churches.

To illustrate again: five hundred years ago one of the three or four most popular subjects of religious art — you see it everywhere in the period: in stone tympani over church doors, in tapestries, in murals, in manuscript illuminations — was the *danse macabre*, the summoning of all men to judgment and, for the most part, the art implies, to condemnation. With no change in the formal theology involved, it is a fact that today that subject has vanished from church art. The glass has changed, cleared or darkened, as you wish, but changed certainly; and with it has changed our "eternity" insofar as it affects church decoration.

Well designed religious buildings take account of such changes. Rooted in eternity, they flower in the moment. We may take pride in them not only as Christians or Jews, but as Christians and Jews of this moment, in this place. Good churches are made for God. They are also made for us; and we are not only rational animals, or humanity, or even the Children of God: we are particular individuals with a certain street address in space, and, as St. Thomas defined "Time," in "the flowing of the Even Now."

It would be pleasant to imagine that the buildings shown here are typical of ecclesiastical building today. It would be deliberately darkening our own glass — even rose color darkens crystal — not to notice two churches unmentioned in these pages but far and away the two most widely known American churches now building: the Cathedral of St. John the Divine, in New York, and the National Catholic Shrine of the Immaculate Conception, in Washington. Whether the Jews have better taste in ecclesiastical architecture or simply the wisdom to be silent about their

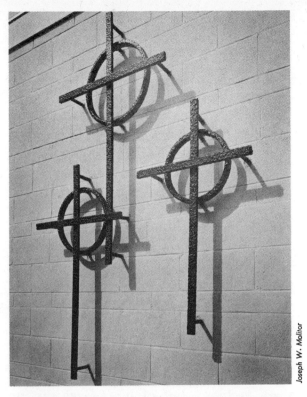

Above: a Head of Christ done in Mahogany by direct carving. Made for Bishop J. Fulton Sheen by Louis Ferrens

Left, top: ornamental crosses in Natick Trinity Church, Natick, Massachusetts. The Architects Collaborative suggested three simplified Celtic crosses to represent the Trinity. Made by a local ironsmith they are hammered wrought iron, galvanized and painted black

Left, center: the altar of the Novitiate of the Jesuits in Plattsburg, New York. Executed by Louis Ferrens, the candles are of wood and polychrome. A silver figure of Christ is mounted on the cross

Left, bottom: a "Menorah" by Seymour Lipton in nickel silver four feet high. Done for Temple Israel, Tulsa, Oklahoma. Percival Goodman, architect

37

mistakes, I do not know; at any rate, there appear to be no extravagant follies on a similar scale.

These two, the one Protestant, the other Catholic, are anachronistic before they are finished. The Catholic shrine, indeed, is only now moving off the drawing board. Plans drawn up 25–35 years ago are now being put into effect. This outmoded conception will be "completed" with a maze of Byzantine towers and Romanesque domes absolutely meaningless to the 20th century. It is true that modifications are being made, but why take half measures? Why not start over? Why not make it a living expression, a building which will command respect?

St. John's, in New York, is in a slightly different dilemma, though the essential albatross is the same bird: a sentimental and expensive dedication to the dear, dead days of long ago. Despairing of ever raising enough money to finish the cathedral in the fifteenth century style to which they'd hoped to become accustomed, the authorities are casting about for ways to solve the insoluble. St. Bernard's line in a letter to Abbot William St. Thierry on the subject of over-ornamentation in churches is relevant: "For God's sake, if men are not ashamed of these follies, why at least do they not shrink from the expense?"

It seems to me that the first requirement of a church or temple today is that it be of today, contemporary, a structure embracing the total life of the parishioner. That parishioner drives a streamlined car to work in an office or factory where everything has been designed for maximum efficiency and comfort. He travels in streamlined trains and jet-propelled planes. Yet every Sunday he is asked to hurl himself back centuries to say his prayers in the pious gloom of a Gothic or Romanesque past. The clear implication is that God does not exist today; He is made out to be a senile old gentleman dwelling among the antiques of his residence, one whom we visit each week out of sentiment and then forget since he obviously has no relation to the normal part of our lives.

God says, "I Am Who Am." This unique use of the present tense abolishes tense itself and sharply rebukes the attempt to imprison God in a granite cell, however lovely the prison windows.

If our work today is to herald a new age in church building, the first step has to be an open minded and modest clergy. In simple frankness, the architectural resurrectionism that blights our church plant today is the direct result of profound clerical ignorance of art and architecture, coupled with boundless clerical self-confidence. Lest the restatement of this plain fact seem presumption in a layman, let me quote a bishop, The Most Reverend Francis C. Kelley, Bishop of the Tulsa, Oklahoma diocese, writing in the *Liturgical Arts Quarterly* for October, 1940: "The fact that a bishop has to examine and approve of architectural plans in his diocese does not make an architect out of him. Gaze on the consequences that have followed the negatives and positives of bishops who were architects only by self-confidence. No wonder we have a liturgical arts movement — we had long needed it. How many are the buildings too costly to replace but too utterly bad to tolerate in silence? Every one of them is a monument to someone's . . . ignorance. The greatest men are those who learn their own limitations. Stubborn men never learn theirs."

The ecclesiastic of any rank cheerfully admits that the laying on of hands has done nothing at all for his knowledge of air conditioning or central heating. He can be brought to see the same of his knowledge of architecture. Help can only come from where the knowledge lies, from the architect or from the well-informed, be he priest or layman. Many Protestant churches have boards of trained laymen who assist the pastor in secular matters; these men, naturally, form the nucleus of any building committee. It is my experience that this lay participation seldom exists in Roman Catholic churches; and yet such groups could be of inestimable aid to the pastor — certainly the businessmen among them could point to the costliness of reiterating past granite glories. The architect should be prepared with periodicals and slides to show the best contemporary ecclesiastical church architecture throughout the world; he should stimulate the thought that architecturally as

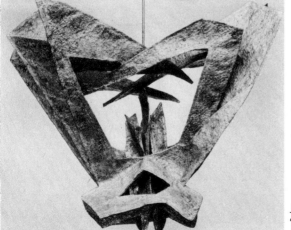

Oliver Baker for Grace Borgenicht Gallery

Oliver Baker

Above: memorial chalice to the late Mother Lucy, Mount St. Scholastica, Atchison, Kansas. The chalice, which is made of silver, was done by Wilhelm Wagner

Left, top: candelabrum by Calvin Albert of lead and lead alloy, 73 inches in height. Done for the Milton Steinberg House of the Park Avenue Synagogue whose architects were Kelly and Gruzen

Left, bottom: a unique lighting fixture by Seymour Lipton for Temple Israel, Tulsa, Oklahoma. Called "Eternal Light," it is made of nickel silver and is four feet high

well as spiritually the church must be the encounter of eternity and the moment.

Religious leaders should realize that the term "modern" is not synonymous with extremism but that just as the Gothic style was a new form clothing an old function, so modern architecture is today.

"It's some new-fangled thing called gothic."

The architect is in a position to say one word in this struggle. The word is "no" said with absolute finality. For, if an uninformed clergy is the source from whom the blessings of ersatz Gothic flow, in every case there has been an acquiescent architect to provide a canal where he should have placed a dam. With great travail, architecture has lifted itself from the brutish trades to professional status. Does that status mean anything at all? What do we think of a doctor who substitutes for his honest diagnosis the sweet words he knows his patient is longing to hear? Is the architect of wedding-cake churches really any different? The architect is indeed an interpreter, the instrument through which his client's dreams are made incarnate. But if those dreams are nightmares, professional honesty requires that they be shown up as such. When the architect has the courage to say "no," more and more ministers of religion will find the courage to say "yes" to his working where he wants naturally to work, in the spirit of the present moment.

A simple device for the long view is the introduction of courses in art and architecture into the curricula of seminaries and theological institutions. If competent instruction was provided — if, for example, instructors were obtained from nearby architectural schools — this delayed action policy could change the face of American church architecture in 50 years.

One special caveat needs mention; beware of the "official" diocesan architect. Almost all who qualify and succeed in this monopolistic spot do so by producing churches of uniform mediocrity.

And one related problem should be touched: church decoration. You cannot destroy the architectural beauty of a good church by embellishing it with cheap artifacts; but you can destroy its effect, for example, by the judicious placement of simpering garish plaster concepts of its great leaders and saints.

Here again, professional help is required and is available. The most competent art advisors, critics, museum directors and their staffs have their offices within blocks of some of the most abominably furnished churches in the world. Eventually, every large congregation, like any good museum, should have an "acquisitions committee" to protect the church from the generosity of donors. The system at Chartres is instructive. Think of the decades through which the St. Sulpice district in Paris has been producing its horrors of devotional art, yet none has ever found its way into the cathedral at Chartres. Why? Because a succession of wise ecclesiastics have placed the real authority in the competent and free hands of the Manury family, now in its third generation of architects in residence at Chartres.

The architect has a continuous obligation to the church he has built. He must, at least, make the attempt to guard the purity of his building. The lay-professional board of a church, of which we spoke earlier, can be helpful here. The new pastor's understandable desire for change where no change is needed can devastate a beautifully conceived interior.

In any region of the country are competent artists ready and willing to help the fusion of eternity and the moment in the work of ecclesiastical art. Their names are available from the heads of our architectural schools and from museum directors. Their employment will do much to enhance churches and to echo once more the plain statement of God that His church is for all men, of all times, in all places.

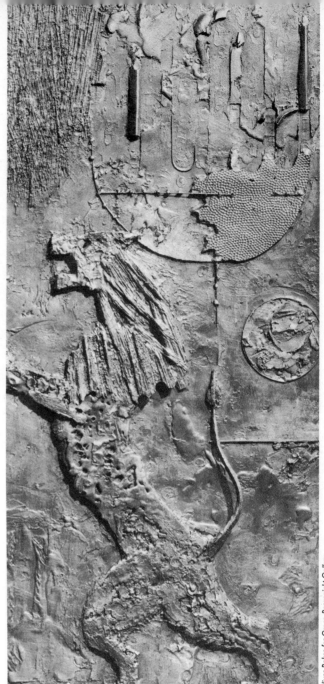

Above: two low relief panels approximately twenty inches wide and four feet high by Calvin Albert. Constructed of lead and lead alloy they were done for the ark doors of the Milton Steinberg House of the Park Avenue Synagogue

Left: a crucifixion of Christ by Hillis Arnold for the house of Mr. and Mrs. McMenemy in New Jersey. The figure is made of glazed terra cotta and is on a walnut cross four feet tall

41

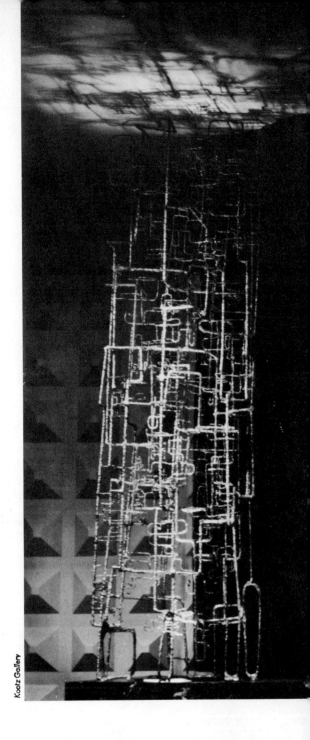

Above: exterior candelabra by Herbert Ferber; opposite Pillar of Cloud and Pillar of Fire by Ibram Lassaw

Kootz Gallery

... JEWISH TRADITION

By Percival Goodman, F.A.I.A.

A FOLK RELIGION based on ethical monotheism. The folk element — a special covenant obtains between God and Israel. The ethics are those of the Decalogue. Symbolic is the *Shema* said on every important occasion, "Hear O Israel: the Lord our God, the Lord is one."

The three divisions of today's Judaism issue from the same source and are fed by the same springs. The differences are not schismatic.

The service of all three consists of prayers, readings from the sacred texts, songs, responsive readings, sermons. There are no mysteries and so the prayer hall should be bright and light.

A choir, concealed or visible, with organ accompaniment, is always part of the Reform service; not a requirement, though often used, among the Conservatives. Instrumental music is never used by the Orthodox.

The liturgical furniture stemming from the tradition (Exodus 25) consists of the *Ark* (focal point generally at the east and containing the scrolls); a covering in the form of a curtain, the *Paroches* (often highly decorated);

a candelabrum located at the right of the Ark; a lamp placed over the Ark "to burn eternally."

The Torah is read from a cloth-covered table. Among the Orthodox and sometimes in the Conservative service, the reader faces toward the Ark; in Reform practice, toward the congregation. There is a pulpit for the rabbi and one for the cantor, or there may be one pulpit used by both.

This furniture is mounted on the *Bema*, (a raised platform). Traditionally this is in the center of the hall, a location preferred by the Orthodox. Both Conservative and Reform place the bema at the Ark end of the hall.

In modern practice a center aisle is provided, primarily for wedding processions, but where the Bema is central there is a space around it.

There is no tradition in architecture or the plastic arts. The architecture is always that of the host country, as is the adornment. However, the Second Commandment proscribes the "making of graven images," so the ornament is either floral or geometric. Equally important, the teaching role of much Christian representational art was unnecessary, for Jews by law had to be literate enough to read the sacred books. In general the proscription still holds, though many Reform Congregations permit representational work.

TEMPLE BETH EL, PROVIDENCE, R. I.

Percival Goodman, Architect
Severud-Elstad-Krueger, Structural
Engineers
Levy & O'Keefe, Engineers
James Douglas Graham, Landscape
Architect
E. Turgeon Construction Co.,
Contractor

ONE OF AMERICA'S OLDEST Reform Jewish congregations celebrated its one hundredth anniversary with the building of this synagogue. Normal seating of a little over 1000 can be expanded to over 1600 for the High Holy days. Complete religious education facilities are included in this building which also contains a nationally famous library of Hebrew and Jewish literature. The social hall is equipped for dramatic presentations and will accommodate over 300 for dinner and over 600 for lectures or plays.

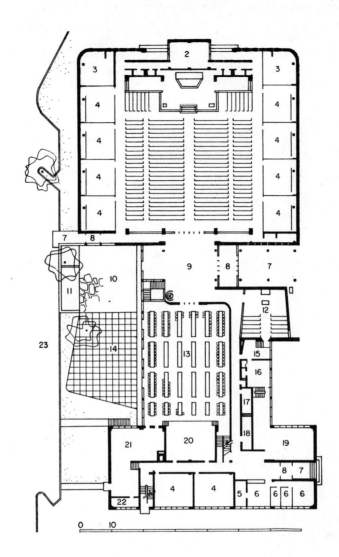

1 TEMPLE
2 RETIRING ROOM
3 CHAIR STORAGE
4 CLASSROOM
5 SUPPLY AND
  MIMEOGRAPH ROOM
6 OFFICE
7 COVERED ENTRANCE
8 VESTIBULE
9 LOBBY
10 TEMPLE GARDEN
11 POOL
12 CHAPEL
13 SOCIAL HALL
14 SOCIAL GARDEN
15 ANTE ROOM
16 RABBI'S OFFICE
17 WOMEN
18 MEN
19 LIBRARY
20 STAGE
21 KITCHEN
22 DRESSING ROOM
23 DRIVEWAY

0   10

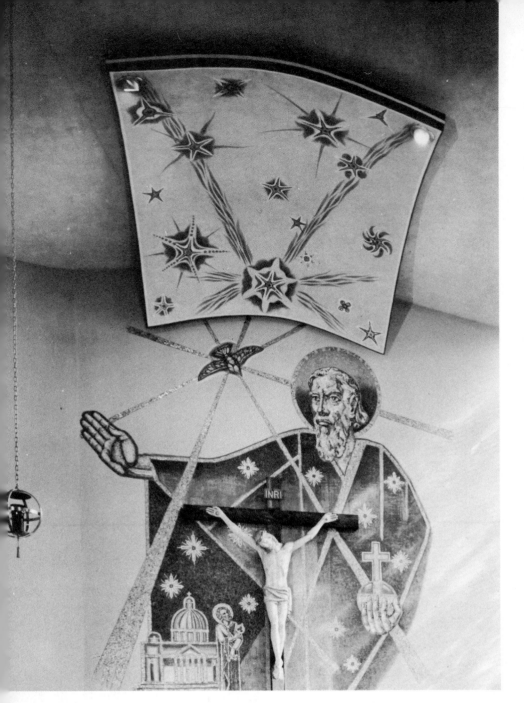

... CATHOLIC TRADITION

By Maurice Lavanoux
Secretary, Liturgical Arts Society, Inc.

THE EVOLUTION of all the arts at the service of religion has now reached a point where we can assess the difficulties which make of architecture in the Catholic Church a matter for concern. The past twenty-five years have witnessed a "cleaning-up" process during which we have gradually been rid of much archeological baggage — a baggage which never had much validity in those days and surely none today.

However, this process has now resulted in a simplicity which bids fair to become another architectural cliché — a cliché of simplicity for its own sake and in which sterility and starkness are the keynote. In the haste to be rid of

meaningless ornament many architects, perhaps too well trained in the school of severe functionalism, have excluded all warmth from their buildings for the Church. They have aped the current clinical *look*.

But in a Catholic church, because of the liturgical requirements and the normal human needs of the average congregation, such coldness is precisely what can be reasonably condemned today. Simplicity is one thing, starkness and sterility is quite another. Fortunately the remedy is within our grasp. It is simply to bring the artist back to our churches; the artist as a responsible person, in which competence is allied to a willingness to work within the discipline of the work at hand. Such discipline, paradoxical as it may seem, really allows the artist full liberty in the exercise of his God-given gift.

The ingredients for a fruitful evolution of all the arts at the service of the Church are simple: liturgical propriety and requirements; architectural simplicity without sterility (in other words, distinguished architecture); all the arts brought into play to infuse the whole with that warmth which makes a church truly the House of God.

(Ed. Note: Mr. Lavanoux's challenge to men of talent: good architecture can develop only out of an understanding acceptance of the conditions and circumstances of the program)

ST. PETER'S CHURCH, PITTSBURGH, PA.

Celli-Flynn, Architects and Engineers
Elwood Tower, Mechanical Engineer
Winterich, Stained Glass, Stations
Rambusch, Mosaic

THE PARISH OF ST. PETER serves 800 families in the South Side of Pittsburgh and its church, seating 750, lies virtually in the shadow of one of the city's large steel mills. The structure is framed in steel and the exterior walls are of insulated cavity brick. Roof is gypsum plank, rigid insulation and built-up finish. Floors are flagstone and ceiling is acoustical plaster. The bell tower is entirely of structural steel with a ¼-in. plate covering the five bell motors. Screen is expanded walkway grating. Cost, excluding only fees and site, was $330,000.

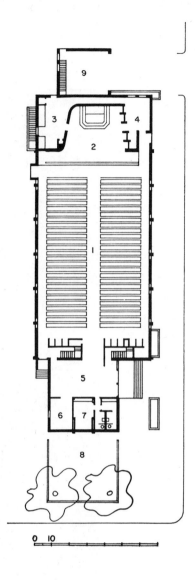

1 NAVE
2 SANCTUARY
3 PRIEST'S SACRISTY
4 BOY'S SACRISTY
5 NARTHEX
6 BAPTISTERY
7 USHERS
8 SHRINE
9 GARAGE

0   10

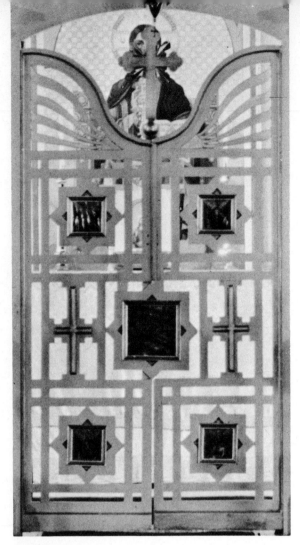

The screen, gate and icons were brought from the former parish church

. . . ORTHODOX TRADITION

By Milan G. Popovich
Rector, St. Sava's Church

IN THE ORTHODOX CHURCHES, church buildings are designed in conformity with the spirit of Orthodoxy as it is expressed in both doctrine and public worship.

The length of every Orthodox church building must follow the east-west line, so that the sanctuary always faces east. A cross embellishes the top of every dome and belfry. It is also profusely used in the interior.

According to Orthodox belief, God is the Eternal King of Heaven, and His symbolic habitation on earth, the church building, should be royal in every respect. The earthly royal splendor has always served as a pattern for the symbolic expression of heavenly glory. The church building should be spacious, richly ornamented, awe-inspiring. The ceiling should be high and curved.

Some churches have a vestibule at the western entrance separated from the nave of the church. Above and across the vestibule, a balcony (choir loft) is built for the choir.

The nave of the church is subdivided into two sections. The rear section, which is very

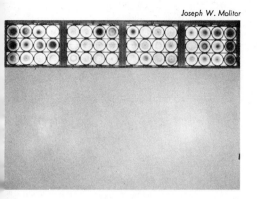

Joseph W. Molitor

Glass roundels were cut from bottoms of bottles blown by Blenko Glass; relief by Ray Smith used same clay as adjoining brick and was fired by same manufacturer

spacious, is assigned for the worshippers. The front section, or chancel, is elevated by one or more steps. It is reserved for the clergy and cantors.

The nave of the church is separated from the sanctuary by a screen called the *iconostas*. It is studded with holy pictures representing the highlights from the life of Jesus Christ and the Mother of God, as well as a number of saints.

Behind the iconostas is the sanctuary, representing the dwelling of the Most High, the Holy of Holies. In the middle of it is a holy table which signifies several things: the table whereon Jesus Christ had His Last Supper,

the cross on which He was crucified, the altar on which the Lamb of God is being sacrificed in the Divine Liturgy, the sepulchre in which He was buried, and the throne of glory upon which He is sitting at the right hand of His Father.

This whole arrangement is designed to conform with the requirements of Orthodox worship, and particularly with the requirements of the Divine Liturgy, which is a mystical and symbolical drama. It represents a re-enactment of the Incarnation and Self-Sacrifice of Jesus Christ, which are correlated with the Creation, Fall and Redemption of man.

51

Joseph W. Molitor

ST. SAVA'S CHURCH, McKEESPORT, PA.

John Pekruhn, Architect
Joseph E. Spagnuolo, Structural Engineer
Charles Hawk, Jr., Mechanical Engineer
Simonds & Simonds, Landscape Architects
Nicholas Le Donne, Contractor

THE SERBIAN ORTHODOX parish of St. Sava's brought with them from their former church a group of liturgical fittings and a strong liturgical tradition. They asked the architect to organize on a hillside site a setting for their worship which would recall for older worshippers the architectural forms of their European childhood and at the same time express the environment and technology and interests of the parish young people. The structure is of steel bents and open web joists, with a copper roof, acoustic tile ceiling and quarry tile floor.

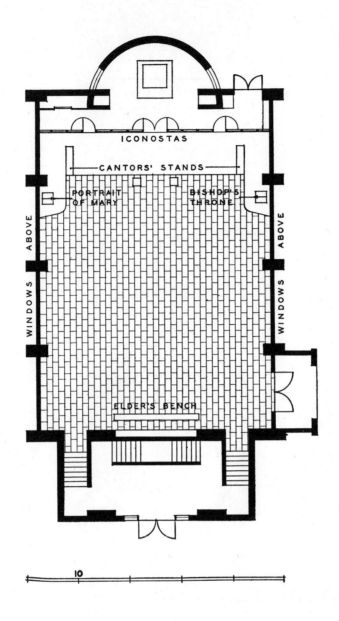

ICONOSTAS

CANTORS' STANDS

PORTRAIT OF MARY   BISHOP'S THRONE

WINDOWS ABOVE

WINDOWS ABOVE

ELDER'S BENCH

10

53

The chancel window was conceived as a color-reredos. Its structural cruciform is embellished and echoed throughout the window which is predominantly blue and white with yellow, ruby, green and copper pink as secondary colors. The window is approximately 350 sq ft

. . . EPISCOPAL TRADITION

By Edward N. West, D.Th., Litt.D.
Canon, Cathedral of St. John the Divine

THE FRENCH MAINTAIN that one may always recognize an Episcopal Church if one finds "the eagle with suspenders." There is a certain justice in this remark since the Episcopal Church, in common with the other churches of the Anglican Communion, is invariably careful to have the written word of God placed in a prominent position, thus the eagle or lectern which holds the Bible is bound to be in a prominent position. The exact liturgics of all the churches of the Anglican Communion presuppose a careful balance between word and sacrament, thus like the early Church, the centrality of the altar is preserved, while the pulpit and lectern

Joseph W. Molitor

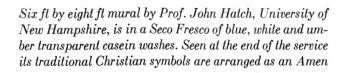

Six ft by eight ft mural by Prof. John Hatch, University of New Hampshire, is in a Seco Fresco of blue, white and umber transparent casein washes. Seen at the end of the service its traditional Christian symbols are arranged as an Amen

are in balancing position in relationship both to the altar and to the congregation.

Although not an ancient habit, crosses will be seen on most of the altars of Episcopal churches. There will, in addition, in most instances, be at least one pair of candlesticks. Full frontals, very long fair linens, and a total absence of lace, characterize most of our churches. In churches where the Sacrament is reserved, more often than not, this will be done in an aumbry or closet, in the north wall of the sanctuary (by north, I mean liturgical north which assumes that the altar is always in the east). Communion rails are now almost universal, but they are regarded as conveniences for the communicants rather than as rails of separation.

There is no such thing as an exclusively Anglican style of architecture. The liturgy will work satisfactorily in any building of any style if it be borne in mind that, from our point of view, a church must be altar-centered with adequate place for the reading and the preaching of the Word, and that convenient arrangements for public baptism must exist.

An architect has only to remember these things in designing a church for us: start with an altar and build a church around it.

(Ed. Note: Compare with Reformed Tradition)

Joseph W. Molitor

*ST. GEORGE'S EPISCOPAL CHURCH, DURHAM, N. H.

John A. Carter, *Architect*
Robert W. Loomis, *Structural*
  Engineer
Robert Sowers, *Stained Glass Designer*
John Hatch, *Muralist*
Ernest R. Sanders, *Contractor*

** Premiated in the 1955 Awards Program of
the Church Architectural Guild of America*

ON THE PRINCIPAL STREET of a small university town a 26-foot high chancel window expresses the worshipful character of this church which seats 150. The church furniture, designed by the architect, the stained glass, and the mural achieve remarkable unity with the pink and gray granite and the cedar of the exterior. The laminated wood arches carry a three-inch plank roof with asphalt shingles. The main floor surface is rubber tile and asbestos vinyl and interior panelling and trim is of pine. Over-all cost was $108,000.00.

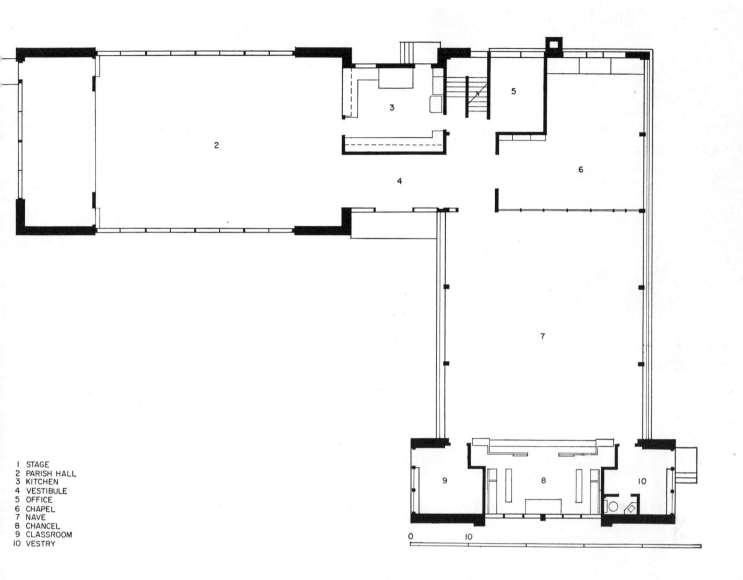

1 STAGE
2 PARISH HALL
3 KITCHEN
4 VESTIBULE
5 OFFICE
6 CHAPEL
7 NAVE
8 CHANCEL
9 CLASSROOM
10 VESTRY

0   10

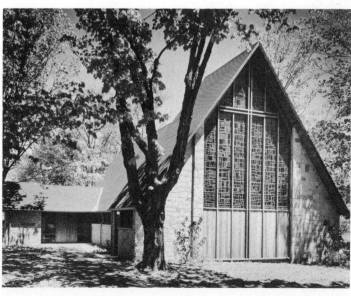

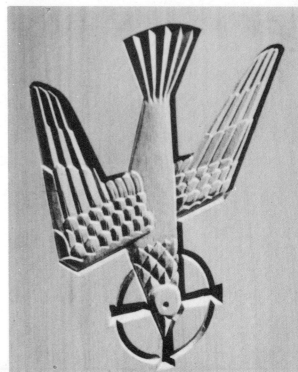

. . . REFORMED TRADITION

By Rev. Marvin P. Halverson
*Executive Director, Department of Worship and
the Arts, National Council of the Churches of
Christ in the U.S.A.*

THE BASIS OF WORSHIP in the Reformed tradition is the recognition of God and what he has done and what he has promised to do rather than man's intentions and hopes. Such worship often has been austere because of the conviction that no physical symbol adequately can represent God in his majesty and glory and love. But it is worship of a fellowship, a community of believers who have been gathered together by God's action. The Reformed churches in New England, which we call Congregational, named their place of worship the "meeting house," for the building was the place where they met each other and as a community met their God.

In the Reformed tradition the sacrament of Baptism is that initiatory act in which a person is recognized as a member of the community. Therefore it has been considered important that Baptism take place before the entire congregation. The other sacrament of the Church is the Lord's Supper. Although it is not observed every week as hoped for and sometimes achieved in the early years of the Reformed tradition, it is central. The Lord's Supper is the celebrational "meal" of the family of God, the Church. Accordingly the Table must be large enough to suggest a banquet around which a large number of persons might gather.

The relationship of the Table to the Pulpit is crucial. The Pulpit, in the language of the earlier years, is the "throne of the Word of God" and the sermon is "the monstrance of the Gospel." Therefore the Pulpit is the place where the Bible is read and the sermon is preached. At the Lord's Table, the Word which is preached is "acted" out as it were, so the Table needs to be related to the Pulpit. Since worship is the act of a community it is necessary that all may see the Table, Pulpit and Font and that all may hear. What is required, then, is a building which enables the Church to worship God according to its understanding of God and His ways with men.

CONGREGATIONAL CHURCH, SPENCER, IOWA

Harold Spitznagel & Associates,
  Architects
Wallace S. Steele, in charge of project
James M. Walsh, Associate Architect
Bolt, Beranek & Newman, Acoustical
  Consultants
Spencer Construction Co., General
  Contractor

THIS SKILLFULLY DESIGNED and detailed church provides a worship center for a middle-sized congregation. Structure employs steel bar joists and laminated wood members. Exterior walls are of face brick and interior walls are variously wood, plaster or brick. Pitched roof is of tile with built-up roof elsewhere. Ceilings use structural fir and acoustic tile. Floors are finished with vinyl asbestos tile. Heating system is hot water with multi-zone ventilating unit in the nave and a radiant system for supplementary heating.

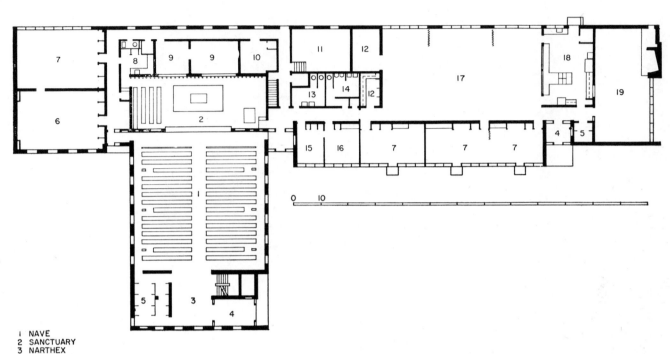

1 NAVE
2 SANCTUARY
3 NARTHEX
4 VESTIBULE
5 COAT ROOM
6 CHAPEL
7 SUNDAY SCHOOL
8 SACRISTY
9 ORGAN CHAMBERS
10 FAN ROOM
11 BOILER ROOM
12 STORAGE
13 GIRLS
14 BOYS
15 SECRETARY
16 PASTOR
17 FELLOWSHIP ROOM
18 KITCHEN
19 FIRESIDE ROOM

Northwest Photographic Illustrators

... LUTHERAN TRADITION

By Dr. Joseph Sittler
Professor, Chicago Lutheran Seminary

"THE WORD BECAME FLESH and dwelt among us." This statement puts one at the central place for pondering what the form of a Christian church should announce. "The Word" is Christ. He is the concretion of what God is, demands, gives.

"The Word became flesh" means that this reality, this saying, this requirement and this gift has occurred in history where men live. The Christian faith is not the bowing of men before a dream of religion; it is the adoration of men before the gracious act of God's Christ given and alive within man's history-house.

"And dwelt among us" means that this new reality is alive here and now. This dwell-

ing creates a community that responds to it, lives by the fact of it, calls itself the very "body of Christ" in the body of this world.

The Lutheran tradition is Christocentric through and through. God is the God who is revealed in Christ. The knowledge of God is what is offered in Christ. The worship of God centers in the entire Christ-deed, from birth through death and resurrection, to His real presence in the household of God, the church.

Therefore every effort to give this tradition palpable, declaratory force must set forth, point to, hold up and draw to the single Christ-center, the multitudinous details of worship. What should be celebrated in both architecture and liturgy is not general religiousness, unspecified spirituality, or a miasmic if potent mood of sheer Otherness. The Lutheran understanding of the Christian faith asserts that all of this is intrinsically unredemptive.

The sole, final and absolutely redemptive fact is God's deed in Christ: Christ in His historical actuality as Jesus of Nazareth, in His real presence as Lord of all things known, received and adored in His church.

(*Ed. Note: This masterful statement places the burden of the formal expression of meaning squarely on the architect; proscribing only the generalized expressions so common today*)

Northwest Photographic Illustrators

CENTRAL LUTHERAN CHURCH, EUGENE, ORE.

Pietro Belluschi and Skidmore, Owings & Merrill, Architects
Cooper and Rosé, Structural Engineers
Donald J. Kroeker and Associates, Mechanical Engineers
Pettengill and Kelley, Electrical Engineers
Albert Vik & Son, General Contractor

THE COMPLETION this year of a nave seating 400 and a chapel for 40 brings to full realization a master plan for this congregation originally conceived by Pietro Belluschi. The parish hall and offices were completed in 1947. Laminated wood arches constitute the principal structural element. Exterior and interior walls are of brick and stained douglas fir. Roofing is built-up. Floors are asphalt tile and carpet. Hot water heating through radiant floor panels. Total cost: approximately $100,-000.00.

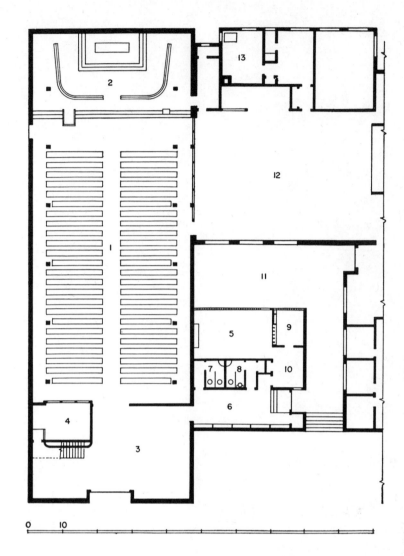

1 NAVE
2 CHANCEL
3 NARTHEX
4 MOTHER'S ROOM
5 CHAPEL
6 COAT ROOM
7 WOMEN
8 MEN
9 STUDY
10 WAITING
11 TREE COURT
12 EXISTING PARISH HALL
13 EXISTING BOILER RM.

0   10

THREE JAPANESE CHURCHES

Antonin Raymond & L. L. Rado, Architects

*St. Anselm's Priory
for the
Benedictine Fathers
in Japan*

ST. ALBAN'S EPISCOPAL CHURCH, TOKYO;
Antonin Raymond & L. L. Rado, Architects.
Located on an open hillside plot of about one-half acre, this church is notable both for interesting structure and for fine handling of natural wood. The double scissors trusses framing the nave, side-aisles and clerestory are made of split cedar poles (half rounds) while the upper wall panels, altar, and altar cross are of contrasting oak. Pews of Philippine mahogany add the richness of a third wood.

The carpentry and furniture were executed in traditional Japanese fashion and with typical Nipponese skill. The fresh-cut, natural look of the surfaces stems from the custom that bars the use of sandpaper on the ground

that its action roughens and "fuzzes" surfaces; softens arrises. Only the saw, plane and chisel are employed, and the finished wood is left completely innocent of stain, filler, lacquer, or varnish.

The handsome trusses and double columns thus become a three-dimensional decorative element. The soft smoothness of the three woods plays effectively against the wire-cut roughness of the orange-red brick in the lower walls and also against the sheen of the polished black asphalt tile floor. Clerestory light is pleasantly softened by white shoji paper patterns pasted upon the glass. Two layers yield two values. They were designed by the architect's wife, Noemi P. Raymond.

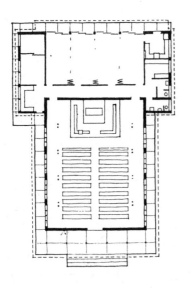

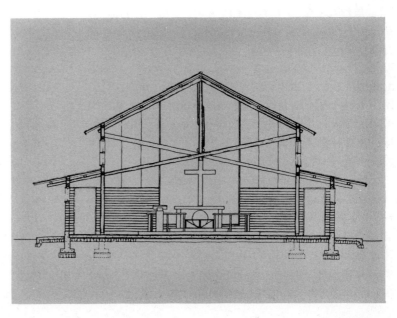

THREE JAPANESE CHURCHES

ST. PATRICK'S CHURCH FOR THE COLOM-BIAN FATHERS, TOKYO; Antonin Raymond & L. L. Rado, Architects. Distinguished concrete work, both rough and smooth textured as well as large and small in scale, lend interest to this building. Also of note is the manner in which multi-colored daylight plays on various interior forms and surfaces to create a softly glowing, three dimensional tapestry.

The concrete structure and walls are natural colored and purposely rough in texture, due to forms made of bevelled boarding. In contrast, the delicacy and precise smoothness of the concrete baldachino (right page) exhibit, in striking fashion, Japanese virtuosity in forming and finishing this material.

For the firm's Japanese work, architect Raymond and his wife Noemi usually work as a team, with Mrs. Raymond determining color arrangements, making sculpture, designing stained glass, mosaics, fabrics, etc.

The floor is concrete, stained orange-red; the pews Philippine mahogany. Clerestory glass panels are in shades of amber, purple, blue, and red while those at the front of the church are in golds and greens. A fresco will someday decorate the altar panel.

The baptistry (upper right) is top-lighted by amber glass. The architect designed the wrought iron screen, mosaic floor, and font. The font is concrete with stone lining; its cover is highly polished black iron.

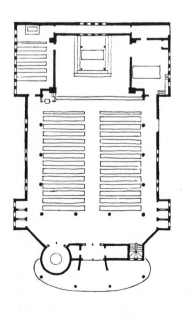

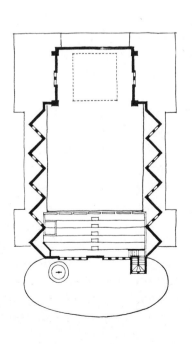

THREE JAPANESE CHURCHES

ST. ANSELM'S PRIORY FOR THE BENEDICTINE FATHERS, TOKYO; Antonin Raymond & L. L. Rado, Architects. Given an unfavorable site, but one on elevated ground, the problem was to design a church for 500, a kindergarten, library, assembly hall and priest's dwelling. The church is flanked on one side by the L-shaped school and assembly facing a play court; on the other by the space set aside for a future cloister and rectory. Covered walks link the elements; serve as corridors.

In the church building proper, there is interest in structure, richness of color, and the extent to which the Raymonds — Antonin and Noemi — participated in the design and execution of all the furnishings.

The side walls and roof are of reinforced concrete in a "folded sheet" form; are laterally braced by the "shelves" between windows in the vertical light strips (pp. 187 & 194). Metal forms were used (for the first time in Japan) and as a result the desired smoothness of surface was achieved. The large nave is in the classic proportion of 50 by 50 by 100 ft. This space creates, for the average parishioner, an effect of serenity and grandeur — a feeling undoubtedly heightened by the manner in which interior color is used.

Portions of the exposed concrete, both exterior and interior, have been dye-stained with transparent washes of color. Since the substance of the concrete remains visible, the

THREE JAPANESE CHURCHES: ST. ANSELM'S

effect is impressive. Earthy colors were used; Indian red, Siena, ochre, gray-green, charcoal gray — and light blue for parts of the ceiling. The large squares in the floor are red and black; the pews and railings are natural Philippine mahogany. The mosaic floor in the baptistry is executed in soft blues and grays.

There is gold lettering on the black stone altar; the flaring baldachino is concrete covered with gold leaf. These were designed by architect Raymond, who modeled the black iron candlesticks; designed and painted the altar tabernacle decoration (top right). This decorative panel is in Cloisonée; consists of areas of baked enamel within raised silver outlines placed upon the black iron supporting frame.

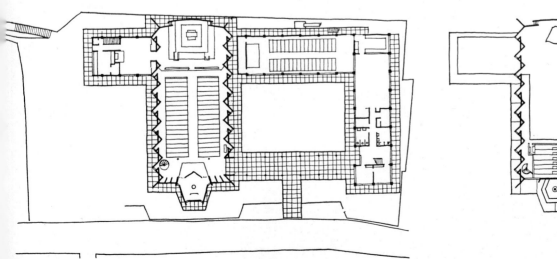

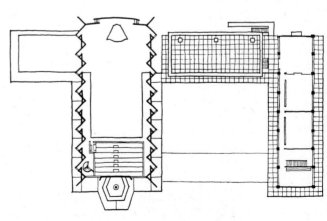

THREE JAPANESE CHURCHES: ST. ANSELM'S

The four top photos show examples of sculpture. The crucifix was modeled by Antonin Raymond and the holy water font — of concrete with a stone lining — was designed by him.

For the stations of the cross, by Noemi Raymond, in all twelve the hands are of black iron while the other elements of the designs are of rusted iron

The two bottom pictures show the spiral concrete stairway leading to the balcony choir loft at the rear of the church

THE HORIZONTAL CATHEDRAL

A discussion with Mario Salvadori on today's structural potentials

WE ARE EVERYWHERE TODAY concerned with finding forms suitable to the purposes of our buildings and to the time and place in which we build them. Our churches have been noticeably slower than other building types in finding forms expressive of their ancient purposes, but at the same time suggestive of the dynamic regenerating force of faith.

However, structural method appears still as valid a source of form as it was in earlier days of great church building and great architecture. The dome was developed in Byzantium and vaulting in Gothic Europe. Is the twentieth century developing forms to rank with these?

There is, perhaps, no one who can answer this question since there are so few who are alive to both structural potentials and the significance of our religions and their symbolism. But it is possible to find among America's experienced and forward-looking engineers answers at least to some questions which are being raised regarding physical values in our evolving structural systems. The editors of ARCHITECTURAL RECORD recently sat down with Mario Salvadori, structural designer and teacher, and questioned him on this theme.

QUESTION: If we continue to experience in our lifetime the revival of religious concern which appears now to be happening, do you see particular potentials that structure gives us which could help satisfy, architecturally, the return of mass interest in religion?

SALVADORI: To date we have seen only a revival of church architecture which may be called the revival for the needs of the individual. It seems that most modern architects who have offered essential contributions,

with meaningful structures, have built only small churches, and most of the time, chapels. For example, the chapel in Belo Horizonte, Brazil, by Niemeyer, which I consider very significant — particularly in terms of its location and its motivations. This revival of interest is taking place and there are a lot of difficulties in trying to materialize it in architectural terms. These small buildings are essentially presenting an individual approach to religion, the approach in which between the person and God there is no room for anybody else. But, inasmuch as the psychological approach used by our culture is of the mass kind, we must inevitably respond to the needs of the masses in religion, and I believe that the only way in which this can happen is by producing structures which will actually embrace a large number of people.

In the Middle Ages massive religious interest produced very large structures. It seems to me that in the future we are going to have the same architectural phenomenon — large structures which will permit the mass gathering of people with the kind of resonance between the feelings of the people which will enhance worship. The essential difference I foresee between the large buildings of the past and the large buildings of the future is this: where the great dimension of the Gothic, for example, was vertical, our great dimension will be horizontal. I believe we now have the physical possibility of doing what other people could not do. In the Middle Ages, if you wanted to have a large group of people in a church, you had to have an essentially tall structure, because in stone large spans demanded large vertical dimensions. We are now in the position of being able to cover a very large area without having great heights. So far, none of our modern architects have experimented in this direction in terms of religious structures. Our only large modern structures whose spaces evoke emotions akin to those called up by the cathedrals are those like the hangars of Nervi and Freyssinet, or buildings like the airport terminal in St. Louis. And if you talk to Nervi, and you see the way he writes about his hangars, you will find a feeling of dedication which is typical of the architect who has an almost religious feeling about the building he builds. Here we have the right psychological state of mind of the architect; here is the need of the people for this new type of religious building; and here are innumerable structural possibilities.

QUESTION: Today what are the several means of this extensive kind of spanning of space?

SALVADORI: We have steel, of course. It is rather strange, but the only cathedrals we have in steel are the old railroad stations like the Pennsylvania train room in New York, which you still see in a few places in Europe, but which are being discarded. The reason is essentially, I think, that they are too costly to maintain.

Then we have concrete. With concrete you can do a variety of things. You can even fake a Gothic cathedral. One of its most interesting uses is in folded plate, or hipped plate, or, as I like to call it, "creased paper" construction. I believe that the potentialities here are very great. One can span distances of 100 to 200 ft with "creased paper" construction and achieve magnificent effect. I have recently seen photographs of a church designed and built by Antonin Raymond in Japan (see Raymond & Rado: "Three Japanese Churches,"p. 67) which is all of this form, and it is very simple and extremely beautiful. If you want to go beyond this, if you want to conceive of the very large cathedrals of the future — really fantastically large and beautiful — in which you would have spans from 200 to 700 ft, the answer is obviously that you have to have curved surfaces. Here we would be going into thin shell design.

Now I believe that in this field Nervi is the one who has really shown us what can be done. His buildings, the large ones, point a direction which is very clear and in which certainly up to 1500 ft, there are almost no practical limitations. Going still further — to a day when we may want to cover areas of say 2000 ft in diameter — I believe you must abandon the idea of a compressive structure, or a shear structure, so you have to abandon both "creased paper" and shells, and you have to go to a tensile structure or a hung roof. Now, if you start using cables and you think of a purely tensile roof, the limits are fantastically high. If you have a cable which can be stressed to only 50,000 lbs per sq in., it can carry itself over a span of about six miles. Of course it wouldn't be able to carry any additional weight, but in the light of this we can easily conceive of spans of a mile. Mr. Viera has shown us that we can now stabilize a roof so that the danger of flutter is completely avoided, and inasmuch as we shall have a little sample of this construction built this summer, I believe we shall be able to find out whether what Viera says is true — and I am sure it is — that no danger of flutter can ever occur. As you know, in tensile structures, it is not the dimension which really stops you. What stops you is that you've got to immobilize the structure.

We are aware that the San Francisco bridge and the George Washington Bridge move sidewise in a strong wind, anywhere between two and six feet. This is perfectly all right, but you wouldn't want a roof over your head that moves six feet.

So the fundamental difficulty in spanning a large distance by means of a tensile structure is the flutter. And it is for this reason that the arena in Raleigh — which in terms of its space is a marvelous building, one of the most successful buildings I've seen — presented serious difficulties. But their problem there has been a problem for the last 30 or 40 years. Paul Weidlinger has a very brilliant solution to this problem. He has a tensile structure which is a sandwich of very thin metal plate which he inflates by a little pressure of air, and in so doing he has a tensile structure which is perfectly steady and will not vibrate.

Caminos has recently devised the lovely looking tensile roof of canvas which could well be adapted to a variety of purposes, including the roofing of churches. But I am not certain that it will be flutter-proof in large dimensions.

I think that on top of the Weidlinger and Caminos solutions, which have not been actually put into practice, we have the Viera solution, and both Paul Weidlinger and I agree that this is the best answer we have today.

The essence of it is this: you have a tensile structure which you overload. You overload it and it comes down a little. Then you put the roofing material on — leaving gaps between the covering elements which would be either steel or slabs of concrete, or other materials. Then, when the overload is put on, you fill the joints. If this is steel, you may put additional plates that you weld; if it is concrete, you mortar the joints. Then you take the overload off. And the moment you take the overload off, the structure goes up again, freezes the compression into the concrete, and the tension in the cables, and it becomes a prestressed inverted thin shell which cannot move, and there is no need for additional elements to tie down the roof as was done in Raleigh. I think that this is the first fundamentally new idea in construction after the invention of thin shells. It's one of those strokes of genius that people have been reaching toward for 50 years. You know, there have been many bright people thinking about it, and they couldn't get anywhere, and here it is.

Viera's Montevideo sports building is 300 ft across, and it costs $1.00 per sq ft to roof.

Now in going back to our cathedrals, if we adopt either the direct solution suggested by Viera, or modifications thereof — and it is quite clear that his principle cannot be modified — I am sure that we can make applications in a variety of ways.

Having solved the problem of flutter, I believe that we can actually span tremendous distances, and that we can have what I would like to call horizontal cathedrals.

QUESTION: Does this mean that with this kind of reversed prestressing idea, you will need fairly strong anchorages of some sort on the sides?

SALVADORI: Well, I'm not so sure of that, you see, because one of the beauties of prestressing is that prestressing is self-contained. You don't need external anchorages to have prestressing. You anchor it to itself. Prestressing is lifting yourself by your bootstraps; for example, in the Viera * solution which I have adopted in the building for Camp Columbia, all these guys and stabilizing cables just don't exist. What I have is a ring all around the building, and the cables are anchored to this ring and put in tension by means of weights. Then we are going to freeze the tension in the cables. We don't need any outside guy wires or any stabilizing wires, because this is prestressing, and is therefore self-contained.

QUESTION: What are you supporting the ring on?

SALVADORI: On just a set of columns. The columns can be very, very slender. Because here is another important point. If you adopt this prestressed, tensile roof, it is a self-contained element, which can be put, like a hat, on anything at all. It could be put on a central column; it could be put on a ring; it could be put on four columns; it could be put on anything you like. You have perfect freedom of support.

I have a ring, I put the ring on top of columns, and I don't need to tie it to the columns. I just put it there. The ring takes it. The ring is self-contained. It cannot buckle. Ordinarily if you have a ring, and you push on it from the outside, it may become an oval, and therefore collapse. But this ring cannot collapse, because in order for the ring to become an oval, one of the diameters would have to become longer while the other becomes shorter.

QUESTION: It is tied across the ring in all directions?

SALVADORI: Yes. It cannot buckle. It's just like a bicycle wheel. I'm going to have a wooden ring, 4 in. by 10 in., to take the whole roof which is 50 ft across.

QUESTION: Would a circular shape always be necessary instead of a square or a rectangle?

SALVADORI: It could be done in a square or rectangular form, provided you admitted some bending on the sides, or provided you used cables on the sides, in which case instead of having a ring you would have a catenary, and then at the four corners, you would have to have the guy wires. The variations are infinite; I foresee a great future for this kind of thing in connection with the large buildings of the type we are discussing.

QUESTION: Along with our need for large religious structures, there will continue to be a need for the small church structure. Some of these principles may be applicable and quite appropriate to these, but in addition are there any particular structural methods we have now or can look forward to that will be useful in small buildings?

Preload Corp. owns world rights to the Viera system.

SALVADORI: It is quite clear that nowadays our structural possibilities are such that we are in danger of running into what Nervi calls "academic structuralism." In other words, the architect knows that he can do anything he likes, and therefore he does wrong things because he can afford to. There are many possibilities that are not even costly. Now in connection with small buildings there is no structural problem. You can use any of the methods we've been discussing here. I believe, for example, that very lovely solutions can be obtained by means of hipped plate, "creased paper" construction in the small scale, or by the continuously curved approach of John Johansen.

QUESTION: You see these as definite improvements over what we actually are using now — bar joists, laminated bents and so on?

SALVADORI: They would be, in my opinion, great advances on two accounts. First of all, it seems to me that when people have been indeed religious, they have expressed their religious feelings by means which had not been used before. When you are deeply in love, and you are a musician, you offer a song which is really new — it must be new because you are deeply in love. And when you deeply love God, and you want to express your feelings for God, you offer something which has never been seen before.

QUESTION: Out of yourself?

SALVADORI: Out of yourself. Now, if you are going to imitate, in a stupid manner, what has been done before, you are not being yourself. Therefore, in one sense, you are not being sincere. And the fact that the modern architect who feels deeply about religion has all these possibilities at his disposal means that the moment we get the right man, we're going to have, even in this small scale, a jewel which represents the integration of his feelings, of form, of structure, of all that makes for a complete expression of religious feeling in the materials of architecture.

Now, for example, I feel that this is what Niemeyer has done in Brazil.

Here is a church which represents the history of the people, represents the countryside, represents through the Portinari mural something the people of Brazil feel very deeply. Yet this marvelous chapel has not been consecrated because the officials of the Church do not feel that it is a religious building.

Now, you have asked if I feel that the conservatism of either the client, or the people, or the architect, would prevent some of these possibilities from being realized. My answer is a most emphatic *Yes*.

It seems to me that if our wonderful potentials are going to be realized, it will not be without difficulties imposed by people, by organized religious groups and their officers. But if the right man gets together with the right denomination, we may have one of these wonderful manifestations soon.

79

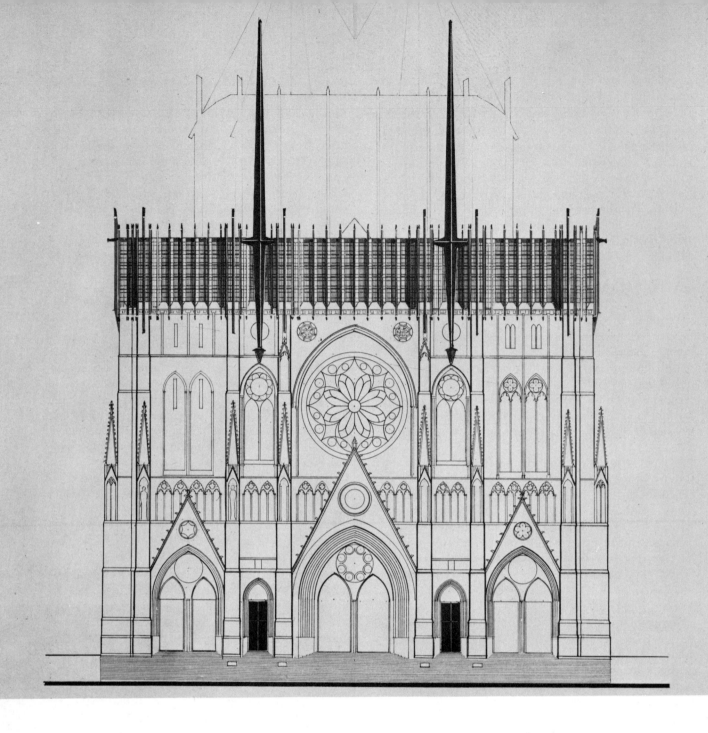

FOR THE CATHEDRAL OF ST. JOHN THE DIVINE

THIS PROPOSAL for the completion of the Cathedral of St. John the Divine was made by John M. Woodbridge in connection with his Master's Thesis in Architecture at Princeton University this year. His general study, of which this was a part, dealt with the problem of relating the new to the old in architectural form. Herewith is the author's description of the way in which he proposes to achieve continuity with the Gothic inheritance through retaining a structural point of departure in which the materials and methods are contrasted.

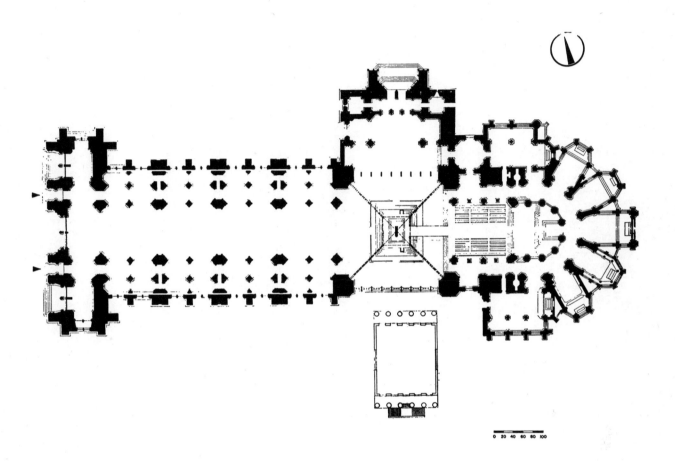

THE INITIAL STEP in the solution was to take account of the existing structural conditions at the crossing, and to place these conditions beside the needs, both esthetic and liturgical, for a powerful setting for the altar in the crossing. The great arches built by Heins and Lafarge to support their tower were the crux of the problem. Cram had virtually discarded them in all of his solutions. But their gigantic scale and the obvious expense of destroying them both argued in favor of keeping the arches if it were possible to integrate them with a contemporary structure. Out of this background came the idea for a tower suspended from diagonal ties within the square of the great arches, an idea which had three powerful reasons in its favor:

First, it provided a natural means of achieving the major aim of the program, the provision of a focal point at a freestanding altar in the crossing, and the tension system could project into the long vista of the interior without blocking it.

Second, it permitted the use of the arches as an integral part of a radically modern structure, combining old and new in a vivid way.

Third, it utilized a structural system which, by expressing lines of force in a way analogous to that of the adjacent Gothic (tension rods and cables with Gothic ribs), provided the op-

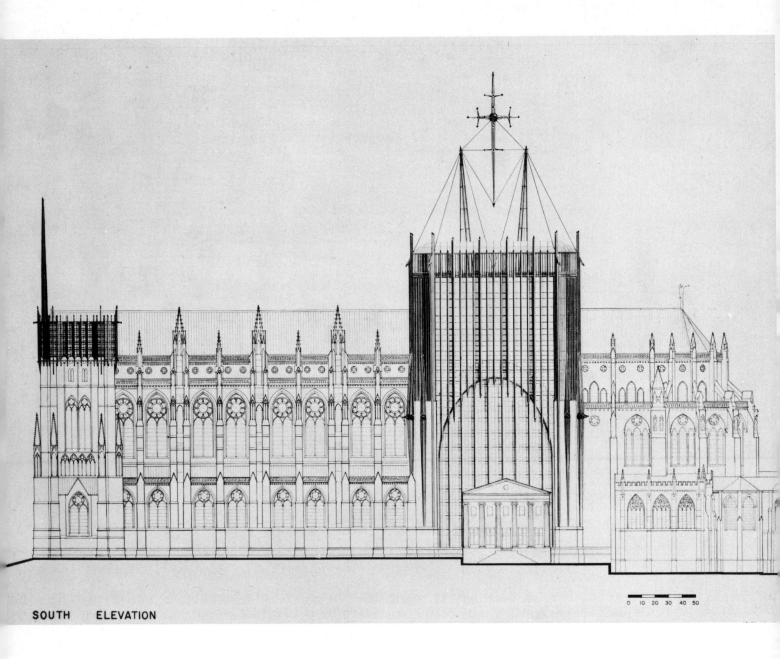

SOUTH ELEVATION

0 10 20 30 40 50

portunity for a structural harmony by contrast.

The scheme involves supplanting the present makeshift buttressing and ties of the arches with diagonal ties across the square supporting four great masts which thrust the ties down into an inverted pyramid centered over the altar. Enclosing the floating tower is a cage structure of concrete slabs and glass built on the arches, providing enclosure against the weather and light control. This cage is designed as an eggcrate with undulating surfaces, deep enough to accommodate the 12 ft thickness of the arches. On either surface of the eggcrate there is a plane of warm-colored diffusing glass bathing the crossing in a high

intensity of warm, diffused light as a contrast with the low intensity of cool light in the other parts of the building. The two surfaces of glass also serve to insulate the great volume of the tower.

Within the side arches is a similar eggcrate of a closer vertical rhythm and smaller depth which would have stained glass on both sides in order to achieve continuity at the ground level with the glass in the existing parts. However, the two surfaces a foot or so apart provide an opportunity for a novel composition in depth, using the two planes to alternate transparent and translucent areas of glass.

The broken surfaces of the cage express the

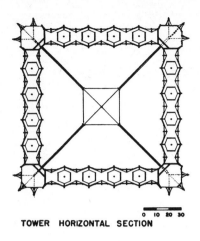

TOWER HORIZONTAL SECTION

0 10 20 30

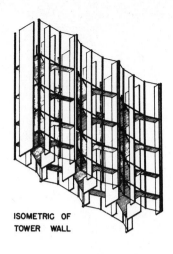

ISOMETRIC OF
TOWER WALL

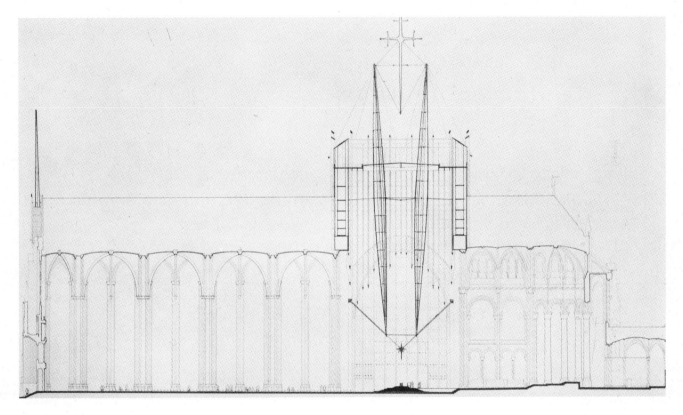

necessity for powerful wind bracing, provide a rhythmic accent in keeping with the rhythm of the buttressing on either side, and break the glass planes so as to achieve an animated surface which insures that the viewer will always be confronted with both a reflecting and a transparent surface.

The roof of the tower is a coffered, polychromed concrete vault with an oculus in the center through which pass the masts. The oculus is intended both to light the interior and to make visible from the interior the separation of the suspended masts from the surrounding cage. As a further expression of the tension system, two crosses are suspended centrally from the tops and bottoms of the masts. A gigantic omnidirectional one above the roof, and one in scale with the altar inside. Apart from liturgical reasons for crosses in these positions, it seems fitting that these two symbolic elements should appear to tie the whole structure together.

There are those to whom a tension system such as this seems inappropriate to a church, but I felt that such a powerful statement of modern structural possibilities was called for in order to hold its own in these surroundings, and there is after all a powerful precedent in the dome of Hagia Sophia, designed to appear hung on golden chains from heaven.

FIRST UNIVERSALIST CHURCH, CHICAGO

*Schweikher, Elting and Bennett,
    Associated Architects*
Frank Klein, Structural Engineer
*Samuel Lewis Associates, Mechanical
    Engineers*
Angelo Testa, Dossal Fabric
*Ashland Construction Co., General
    Contractor*

THE FORM OF THIS CHURCH is a response to a non-creedal, liberal congregation's needs on a restricted, urban site.

Seating for 140 in the sanctuary, 20 in the choir and 40 in the balcony accommodates the relatively small membership of the only Universalist Church in Chicago.

Solution to the problem of shutting out the confusion of the city without repelling the public was found in surrounding what is actually a pair of buildings with a brick wall which in part forms the building exterior.

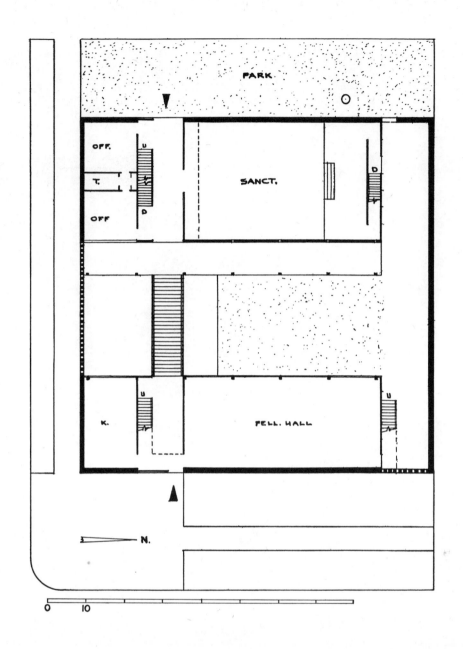

PARK.

OFF.

SANCT.

T.

OFF

K.

FELL. HALL

N.

0   10

Hedrich-Blessing

An invitation to the passerby is offered through the two large glass areas and the open brickwork.

The building's overall character may be well understood against the background of quotations from a statement on Universalism by the church minister, David H. Cole:

"Truth comes from many sources, chiefly through use of the scientific method rather than solely from Biblical authority.

"Universalists are unitarian in theology, revering Jesus as an inspirational leader, human as other men, and divine in the sense that all men are divine.

"Salvation for Universalists is a matter of growing toward individual maturity and working together for a democratic society of brotherhood and peace."

Structural system consists of bar joist floors and roofs carried on bearing walls of cavity insulated brick and on steel columns.

Major materials are Belden brick, concrete slabs, gypsum roof decks and plaster or stucco screen walls.

Heating from a single boiler is by forced warm air in sanctuary and offices and finned tube steam radiation elsewhere.

Square foot area of the building is 10,430; cubage: 121,970. Completed in 1955 the cost was $135,000.

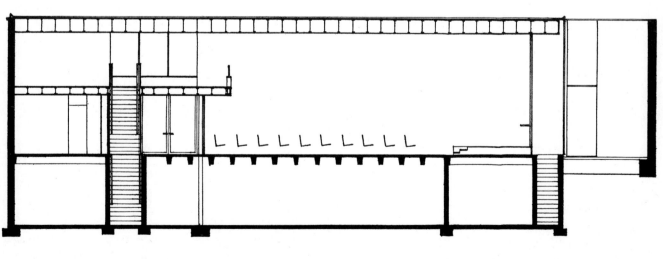

0   10

FIRST PRESBYTERIAN CHURCH
4785 SHANKLAND RD.
WILLOUGHBY, OHIO

87

JEWISH CENTER OF WEST ORANGE, N. J.

Davis, Brody, Juster & Wisniewski,
*   Architects*
Beck, Simon and Mantel, Structural
*   Engineers*
G. Robert Goodall, Site Consultant

THIS BUILDING IS actually a community center in which religious, educational, and social facilities have been provided for round-the-week use.

Principal problems were organization of the various functions into an economical and flexible building and the creation of a religious atmosphere for the chapel distinctly apart from the rest of the building's uses.

The chapel seats 250 and is expandable to 350 by using the foyer. The multi-purpose room — normally employed for social and edu-

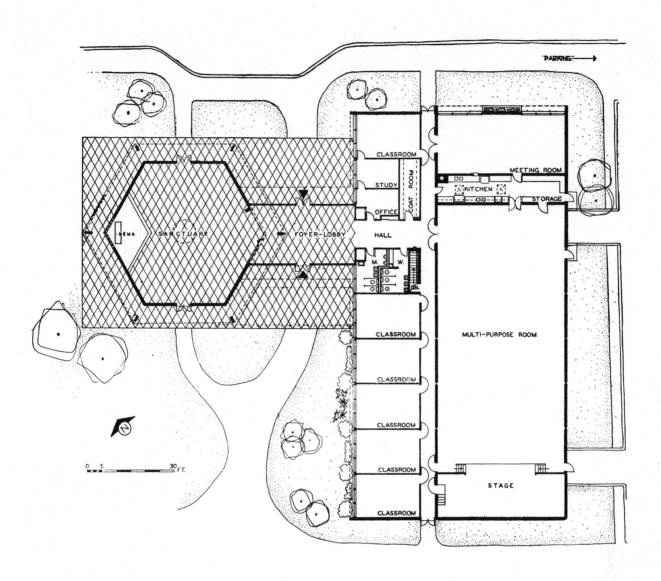

SANCTUARY

BEMA

FOYER-LOBBY

HALL

CLASSROOM

STUDY

OFFICE

COAT ROOM

M. W.

CLASSROOM

CLASSROOM

CLASSROOM

CLASSROOM

CLASSROOM

MEETING ROOM

KITCHEN

STORAGE

MULTI-PURPOSE ROOM

STAGE

PARKING

N

0 5   30 FT.

cational gatherings — can seat 750 for religious services on the High Holy Days.

The structural system in the chapel makes particularly handsome use of laminated wood arches and brick cavity walls. The roof here employs 4" wood decking as it does also over the classrooms, the meeting room and the foyer where it is carried on wood beams bearing on stud walls and marble faced block cavity walls.

The multi-purpose room is framed in steel using long span joists, composition decking and marble faced block cavity walls. As used here, the white marble faced block is an economical and attractive material.

Other principal materials are the buff manganese spot brick used inside and out in the chapel which has a wood ceiling and terrazzo floor. The same ceiling and floor materials are used in the foyer.

In the classrooms mahogany plywood faces the interior walls, the ceilings are wood and the floors are asphalt tile. The multi-purpose room uses a hung, perforated, white-enamelled, aluminum acoustic ceiling and maple flooring.

Heating in the multi-purpose room is by means of six hot water unit heaters in the hung ceiling, delivering through anemostats and fan-exhausted at the stage end. Elsewhere heating is through wrought iron floor coil.

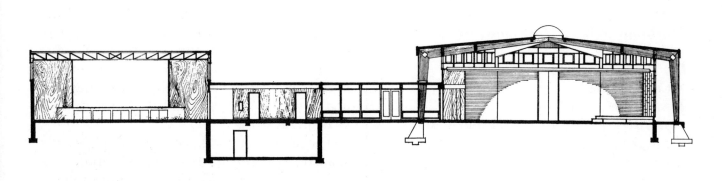

Hedrich-Blessing

ST. ANDREW'S CHURCH, PARK RIDGE, ILL.

Charles Edward Stade & Associates,
Architects
M. Dolan and H. Anderson, Associated
Architects
Dr. A. R. Kretzmann, Liturgical
Consultant
John Torell, Sculptor
Clark Engineering Co., Mechanical
Engineers

THIS SUBURBAN LUTHERAN church is a carefully detailed and well executed example of an approach to design which is on the generally conservative side of current efforts. Serving a middle-sized congregation, the combined seating totals 590 using both the meeting area at the rear of the nave and the church parlor as overflow areas.

The site is a level, corner lot, pleasantly shaded by maturing trees and generally free of difficult design determinants except for a busy highway that influenced the retired posi-

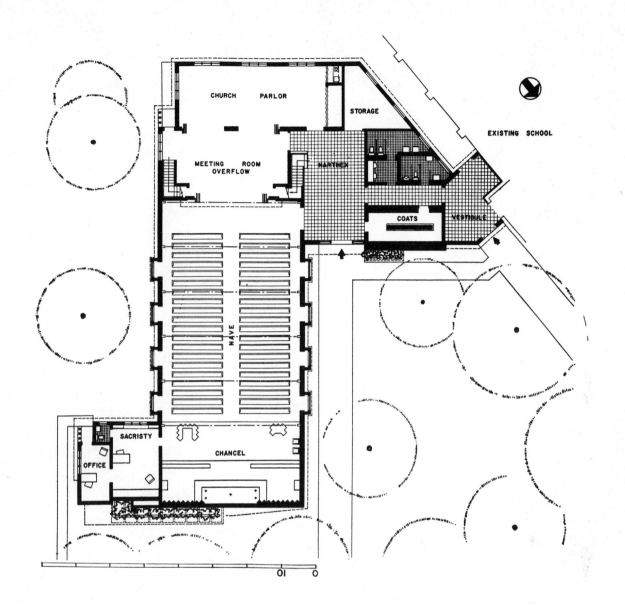

CHURCH   PARLOR

STORAGE

EXISTING SCHOOL

MEETING   ROOM
OVERFLOW

NARTHEX

COATS

VESTIBULE

NAVE

SACRISTY

OFFICE

CHANCEL

tion of the main entrance. The total effect of the natural, and unusually rich, materials is most effective.

The roof structure is of exposed laminated trusses, purlins and beams carrying 2″ x 6″ T & G "V" joint fir planking. Walls are generally of face brick on both exterior and interior. Roof surface is asbestos shingle.

Cathedral glass is used in the high windows of the nave. Artificial illumination is furnished from concealed cove lighting and the suspended brass fixtures.

The architects have tried to focus principal attention on the large brick and stone altar and on the 21 ft carved oak cross. The three plaques at the foot of the altar are also of oak as is the panelling in the sacristy.

The reinforced concrete slab floors are finished with asphalt tile. Sash, frames and doors are in wood; gutters, downspouts and flashing are copper. Rigid insulation is used in both exterior walls and on the roof. The exterior siding is redwood and in common with all wood surfaces inside and out is merely stained and protected. Some color accent is used under the eaves and on the doors.

Heating is by means of an oil-fired boiler; radiant hot water coils in a floor slab installation combined with wall convector radiation.

Total cost of the building was $151,000.

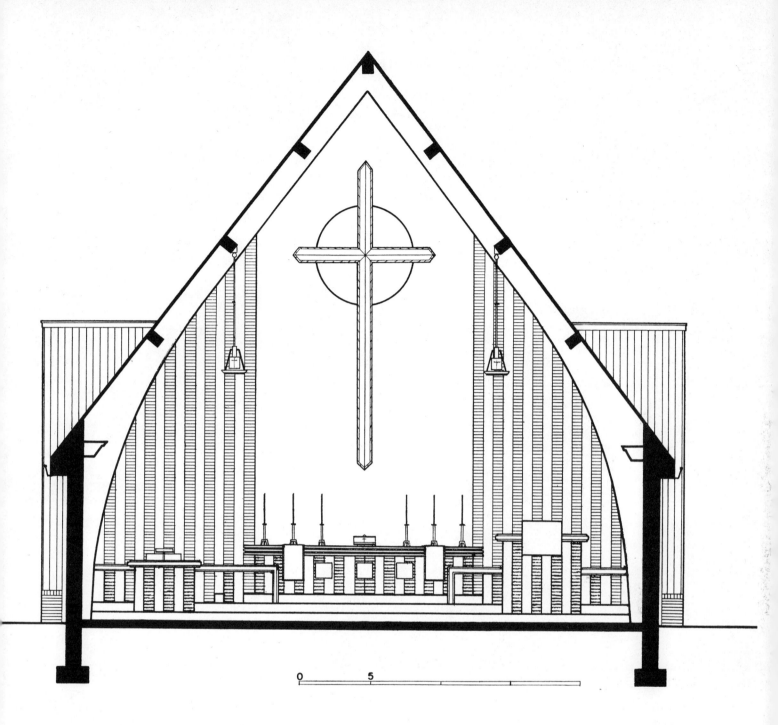

95

ST. FRANCIS OF ASSISI CHURCH, WESTON, CONN.

Joseph Salerno, Architect
James Fanning, Landscape Architect

THE CENTRAL FACT of Catholic worship is the altar, the table of sacrifice. In this church, the aim has been to express this idea as clearly and emphatically as possible. Roof and wall all incline toward the center. The variations in natural and artificial light help to accomplish the same thing with the brightest source in the glass steeple over the altar.

Since nowhere does the roof rest directly on the walls the sense of a floating ceiling is provided.

The orientation of the building provides

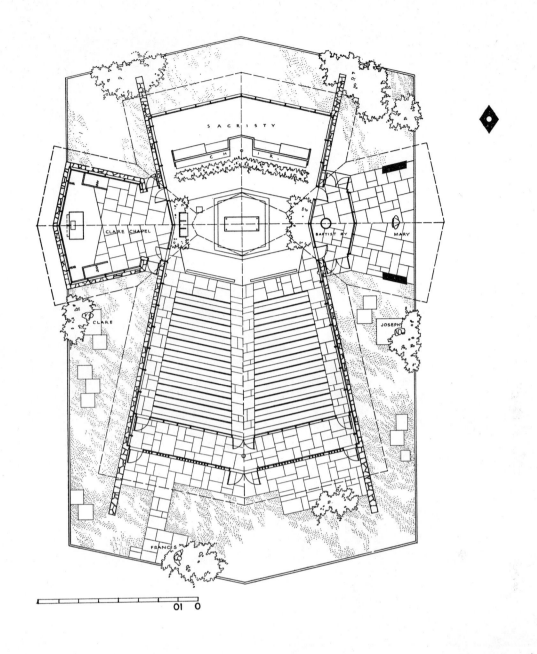

SACRISTY

CHOIR

CLARE CHAPEL

BAPTISTRY

MARY

CLARE

JOSEPH

FRANCIS

01   0

P. E. Guerrero

light from the back of the congregation for morning Mass. The subdued colors of fieldstone and wood contrast with the white granite of the altar and sanctuary floor.

The amount of space given to the sanctuary and the liturgical position of the choir is unusual, and interesting. Mass may be celebrated facing the people. Planting in the sanctuary is in honor of the patron, St. Francis of Assisi.

The Clare Chapel serves for reservation, for daily Mass, small weddings, for confession and for small children at Sunday Mass. All sculpture, with the exception of the suspended crucifix over the main altar and the crucifix in the Clare Chapel, is outside the church. Stations of the Cross will be in stained glass windows contained in the seven bays of the main body of the church. The east wall is designed to be demountable for expansion.

The church is the first building in a group which will include rectory, convent, school and parish hall.

The building was designed under the direction of Msgr. Joseph F. Cleary of Sacred Heart Church in Georgetown, Conn., and his cooperation, along with that of Father Corrigan and Bishop Sheehan of Bridgeport has been notable in the area of architect-clergy relationships.

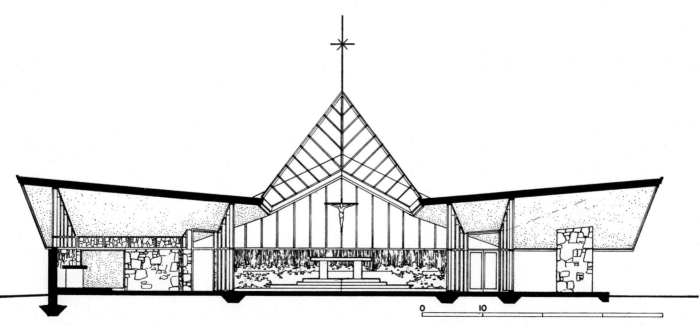

PILGRIM LUTHERAN CHURCH, BELLEVUE, WASH.

Grant, Copeland & Chervenak,
  Architects
Stern & Towne, Mechanical Engineers
Howard Johnson, Electrical Engineer
R. C. James, General Contractor

THE PROBLEM HERE involved the design of a building for a new mission congregation in a rapidly growing residential area on the eastern shore of Lake Washington.

The trapezoidal site is about one mile from a small business district and because it is relatively low-lying demanded a membrane slab.

On a budget of $30,000 the architects were asked to provide seats for about 140 and some method of handling overflow attendance. Here, as in many formative congregations, the archi-

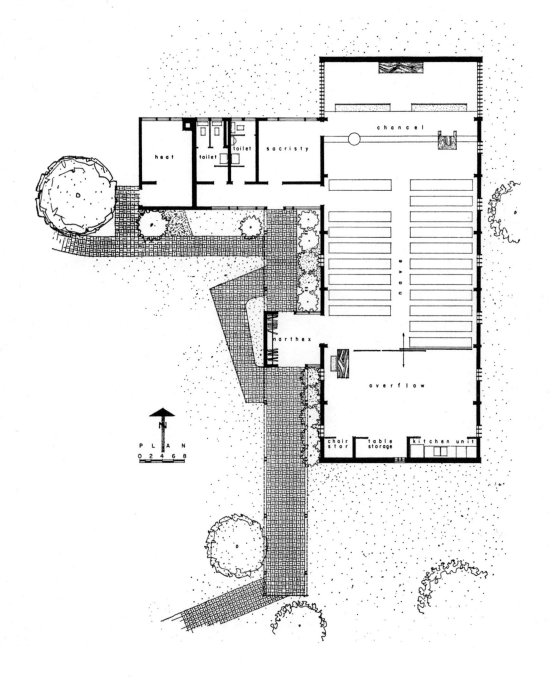

PLAN
0 2 4 6 8

heat · toilet · toilet · sacristy · chancel

nave

narthex

overflow

chair stor · table storage · kitchen unit

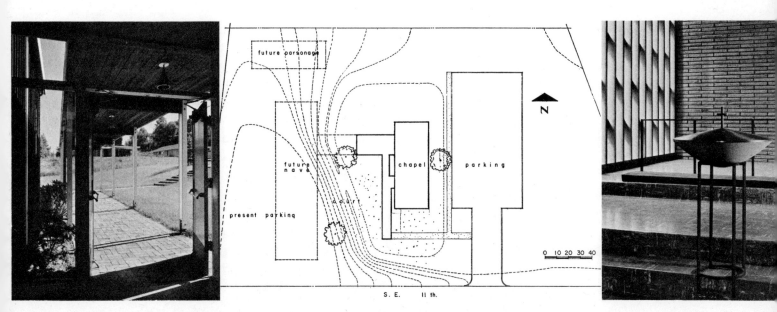

future parsonage

future nave

court

chapel

parking

present parking

N

0 10 20 30 40

S. E. 11 th.

Dearborn-Massar

tects had to design a suitable worship space that would, in time, become an all-purpose parish hall and educational facility. For the time being all activities take place in the temporary nave and are organized by means of a large screen which rolls forward to permit parish activities in the rear and by L-shaped nesting screens which divide classroom spaces there.

The structure consists of glued-laminated arches with 3 x 6 fir "V" joint wood decking for the ceiling and roof construction. Nave walls are 2 x 6 studs with 1 x 8 cedar boards both inside and out where 2 x 3 battens cover the joints.

The full height nave windows are glazed in reds, greens, blue-greens and purples.

Interior colors are stained shades of brown and ivory, accented by the dull black mild steel elements of the communion rail, font and pulpit whose top is white birch. The font is cast stone with a spun copper cover and a copper cross. The altar is faced with travertine.

Exterior siding is stained a warm brown with columns, trim and facias painted white. The roof is covered with white marble chips.

The contracted cost of the chapel was $28,-500 or about $10.68 per sq ft. Brick sidewalks, interior staining and painting were donated by the members.

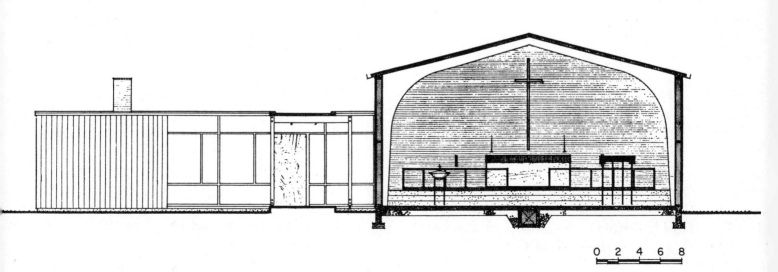

0 2 4 6 8

INTERDENOMINATIONAL CHAPEL, MIRAMAR, CALIF.

Richard J. Neutra and Robert E.
*   Alexander, Architects*
Dion Neutra, Robert Pierce, Howard
*   Miller, Richard Stadelman, Benno*
*   Fischer, Sergei Koshin, John*
*   Blanton, Toby Schmidbauer, Perry*
*   Neuschatz, Gunar Serneblad:*
*   Collaborators*
Parker and Zehnder, Structural Engrs.
Boris Lemos, Mechanical Engineer
Earl Holmberg, Electrical Engineer
D. J. Free, Acoustical Conslt.

THE PROGRAM for this chapel asked for 600 seats plus an additional 120 for religious education and the morning chapel.

The plan was dictated by the site and by such special requirements as the rotating and disappearing altar which has been designed to serve Saturday and Sunday schedules for the interdenominational use of the community.

Structure of main chapel is of precast concrete arches and wall panels, with gypsum roof and hung plaster ceiling. Other structures are of concrete block with wood roofs.

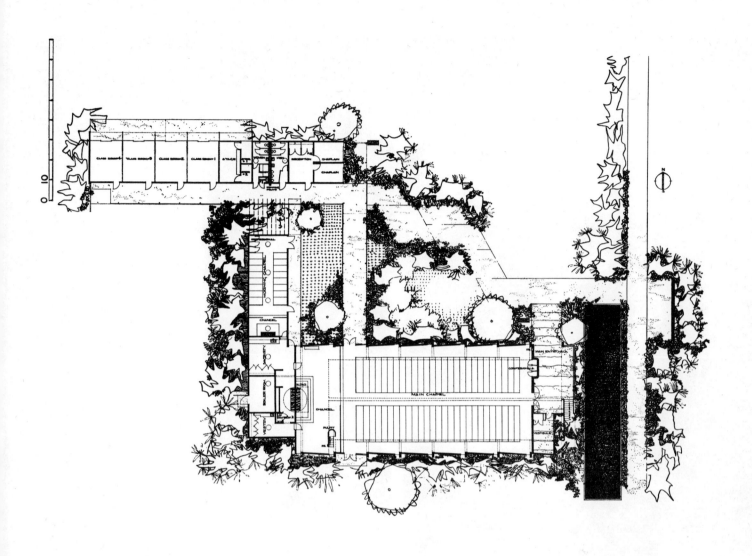

FROM THE ARCHITECT'S OFFICE:

The architects feel that the western and in fact most religions have in common the need to express a processional, or dynamic "moving forward," toward the altar or focus of worship. Mr. Neutra, in his book "Survival through Design," has pointed out the physiological basis of ritual patterns as well as of all human behavior. The architect must be interested in this in order to serve man right, whenever and wherever it is.

Space is the great universal experience of man and it has for man its deep cargo of religious feeling. But this is not geometrical space rationally and abstractly analyzed by Euclid. It is space experienced through all our millions of sense-portals and with all our inner being. Apart from the indifferent Euclidean Space, the vibrant, sensory experience of it is *directional*. It has an up and down, a forward and something overcome and left behind.

Nature has set our eyes in the front of our head; it is no indifferent accident that our arms

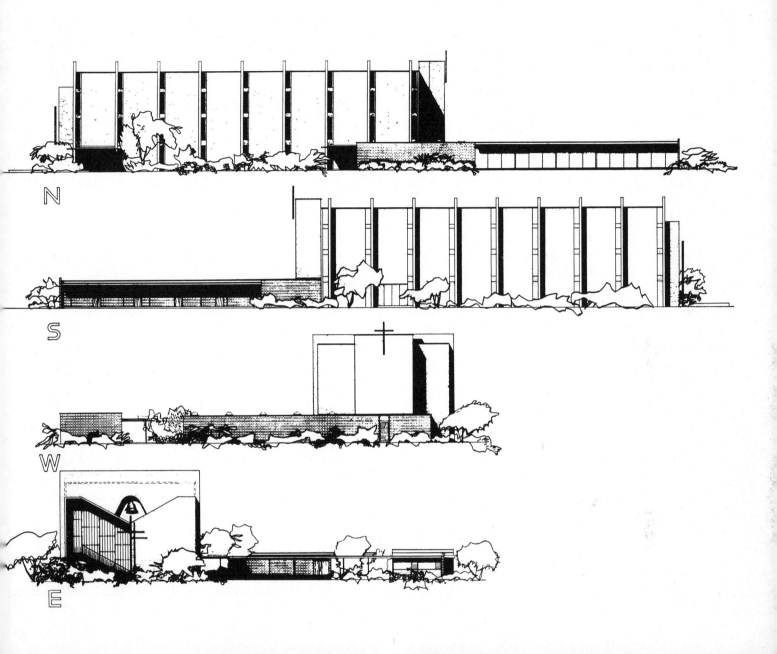

N

S

W

E

are jointed to be raised forward and our legs carry us where our vision leads. Our entire nervous makeup puts emphasis on direction and direction in space has acquired spiritual accent through one hundred thousand years, and later from Luxor to Chartres.

In addition to the natural forward move horizontally there should also be expressed an upward or heavenward tendency, which must be, by necessity, mostly visual. This feeling should impress itself on the visitor the moment he enters the church, and preferably he should be aware of it even before he enters.

The concept of this church creates this feeling in a way which will be kept in the memory of the onlooker. Starting with the outside, we see a symbolic bell, as has been used for convocation through many centuries. The bell is silhouetted against an interestingly translucent opening which is illuminated at night. This opening is seen over the valley formed by the inverted "V" — an expressive shape — of the ceiling as extended to the exterior of the building. From one side of the ridge is supported a unique hanging stair which, by its upward slant, symbolizes spiritual ascent. A glass screen is all that separates here the interior and exterior, so as to make this entry to a higher plane as inviting as possible.

The main nave entrance is approached through an open archway below the balcony into an interesting covered porch or vestibule. From here one can choose either to ascend the stair to the gallery, or enter the nave.

Immediately on entering, one feels the impression of the upsurge mostly through the shape of the massive concrete frames on both sides which tend to arch over but disappear behind the ceiling, high above, as if over clouds. The only natural light sources occur,

concealed, forward of each frame. Being thus shielded, they will spill light toward the altar but not toward the observer looking forward. The shape of the floating ceiling, being higher at the edges than at the center, will seem to soar upward. But also the ridge of this ceiling, starting low over the balcony, rises and, especially when lighted, guides the eye upward and forward toward the altar.

The altar itself is illuminated by an inconspicuous, rather concealed, continuous skylight across the entire width of the nave, returning down the sides of the chancel or pulpit platform.

An unusual, dynamically graded division of the plastered rear wall of the altar heightens the perspective effect and gently emphasizes the spiritual importance of the altar wall, toward which all the directionalism of the design converges.

Vestment and sacristy rooms are grouped behind the chancel and altar, with convenient access for services to the main chapel and the more intimate morning chapel.

The main court or patio of the chapel is formed by the long wall of the chapel on the south, the cloister of the morning chapel on the west, and the main pedestrian approach walk on the east. Access to the chapel by car is from the west to an ample parking lot, where auditory disturbance is removed from the church goer, and then past pleasant Sunday-school class-rooms opening in a friendly way onto nature and onto their own outdoor landscaped patios. The main cloistered courtyard seems to follow an early California pattern.

Faint night illumination of the exterior of the chapel from below, and of its grounds, is planned so that at all times this spiritual focus of a community never disappears.

All photos by Julius Shulman

CHAPEL OF THE HOLY CROSS

Anshen & Allen, Architects; Robert D. Dewell, Civil and Structural Engineer; Earl & Gropp, Electrical and Mechanical Engineers; William Simpson Construction Co., General Contractors; Fred Coukos, Construction Superintendent; Bernard T. Espelage, O.F.M., D.D., Bishop of Gallup; John Driscoll, Pastor; Keith Monroe, Sculptor

The Chapel of the Holy Cross at Sedona, Arizona is an arresting building. It is also fine architecture. It combines more than the usually requisite assortment of identifiable satisfactions in such a way that the total effect renders analysis of its particulars, though pleasurable, an academic process only partially instructive because it is incapable of completion.

Of course all fine architecture resists analysis. Here, for example, it is possible to identify the particular ingredient of an unparalleled site; to recognize in the shape and scale of the building and its parts, in the choice of surface, color and texture the sensitive respect which the architects have expressed for the character of that site and at the same time for the particular functions and materials and processes involved.

These are causes and effects capable of sensible amplification. But beyond the ability of words to describe its achievement, this building can speak to the mind and spirit regarding place and time and purpose. Certainly it suits its site. It has the ability to suggest today, both yesterday and tomorrow, and it is an architecture appropriate for worship with power to impress its expressive image on the memory.

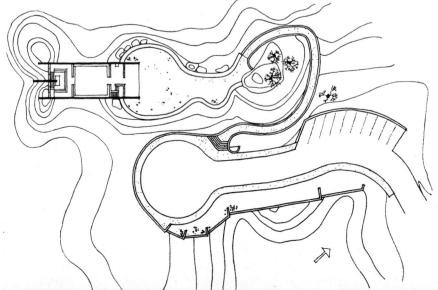

THREE MILES from Sedona, Arizona and one hundred fifty feet above the floor of the Verde River Valley, the chapel rises from a spur of deep red sandstone at the base of a fifteen hundred foot vertical cliff graduated in color from the red of the spur to a light cream top.

From the car turn around below and east of the chapel, steps lead to the textured concrete ramp, which curves up and around the cliff of the spur to the chapel entrance plaza.

The chapel itself, the gift of Marguerite Staude to the Roman Catholic Church in memory of her parents, is designed to seat approximately fifty people in the permanent pews along the side walls and across the rear. In the months when tourists may swell the size of the congregation, folding chairs will increase the capacity to one hundred fifty. In the basement are the confessional, office, two sacristies and services.

The building is a reinforced concrete shell, twelve

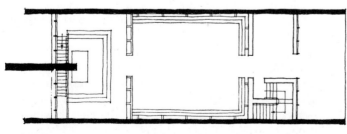

MAIN LEVEL

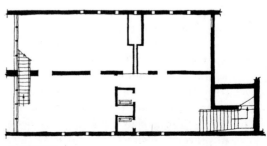

LOWER LEVEL

inches thick, integrally colored and sandblasted to expose a rich textured aggregate on both the interior and exterior surfaces. The walls were poured in sections, eight feet high. The two ends of the chapel are glazed with a smoke colored glass which eliminates glare while permitting a clear view of the magnificent panorama beyond the altar. The orientation to the southwest and the projecting side walls and cross act as a large louver in preventing direct sunlight from falling on the glass.

The floor surfaces are trowel-finished concrete. The tall, slim entrance doors are aluminum with specially detailed horn-shaped handles.

Construction was carried out under most difficult conditions and the architects are particularly grateful to the general contractor and his job superintendent for the high quality of the work. Interestingly the contractor as a young man had built the church which is the headquarters for the chapel pastor.

The great cross in the southwestern end wall is ninety feet high and carries on its interior face both the black marble altar and the Corpus. This fine piece is the work of Keith Monroe, San Francisco sculptor. It is wrought in iron and like the building as a whole strongly reflects the rugged environment. It is thirteen feet high and its rough highlighted shell surface is in strong contrast with its dark hollowed interior spaces.

Taken all together, this building is a transcendant integration which seems to draw its strength from its location, from the simple freshness and suggestion of endurance in its profile, the rigorously restricted palette of materials, the recall of environmental elements without actual use of site materials, the skillful contrast of the curvilinear ramp and plaza with the crystalline contours of the building, and most importantly the precise organization of parts to achieve an impression of size which is in harmonious scale with the grand setting.

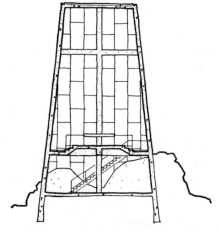

It may fall to the lot of other architects to work with sites of similar grandeur, if plans for the Mission 66 program of the National Park Service do lead, as planned, to a substantial building program in the national parks. NPS and its concessioners in the parks will be dangling before architects just such problems in scale, in awesome scenery, color, lighting conditions.

In an earlier day rusticity was the accepted answer, or chalet importations from another mountainous land. Contemporary architecture has not had much opportunity to test its tenets in such terrain, or, too much success when it has had the chance.

The design of this chapel seems to suggest a better approach than we are used to in our national parks. The chapel does not seem bothered by the problem of scale. It does not seem to feel called upon to feign modesty, or to bow to the hills in feeble imitation. Nor does it try for self-assertiveness in the manner of a bantam rooster. It seems rather to appreciate its magnificent setting. and react like a well-mannered guest.

LE CORBUSIER'S NOTRE DAME DU HAUT AT RONCHAMP

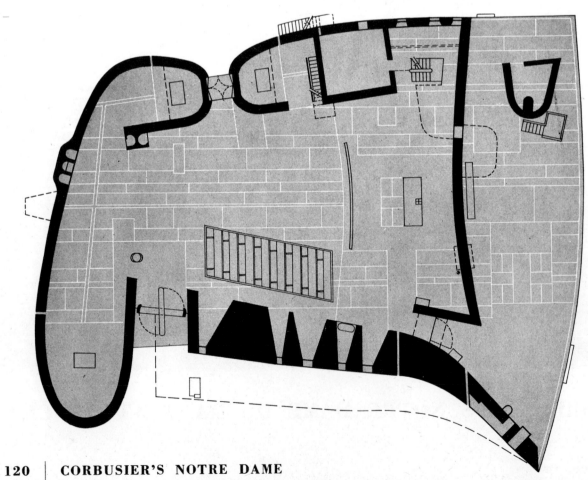

JOHN SHEAR

PARIS

ARCHITECTURAL RECORD
NEW YORK

CORBU HAS MADE GREAT PROGRESS IN ARCHITECTURAL COMPOSITION. NOTRE DAME DU HAUT CHAPEL IS HIS BEST. DOUBTS CREATED BY ALL PUBLISHED PHOTOGRAPHS COMPLETELY ERASED BY ANALYSIS "A PIED D'OEUVRE." BERNINI'S AND BORROMINI'S TOOLS WERE USED BY CORBUSIER AS 13TH CENTURY ONES WERE USED BY PERRET AT NOTRE DAME DU RAINCY. GOOD ADAPTATION TO SITE AND LIFE WITH SAME BASIC TOOLS USED IN SANCTUARIES BY GREEKS, MAYANS, CHRISTIANS, ETC. EVERYTHING IS THERE INCLUDING CORBUSIER'S SIGNATURE BY FINGERPRINTS NEAR THE SYMBOL OF THE VIRGIN MARY. UNFORTUNATELY CROSS AND CHRIST WITHIN CROSS PERFECT EXAMPLE OF ARCHITECTURAL ANTI-CLIMAX YET ELEMENTS OF COMPOSITION ARE MAGNIFICENT EXAMPLE OF MONUMENTALITY WITHIN MINIMUM PHYSICAL SIZE. RONCHAMP EXPRESSES A LIBERATION OF CORBUSIER FROM CORBUSIER.

LABATUT

Prof. Jean Labatut, Director of Graduate Studies, School of Architecture, Princeton University, visited Ronchamp on behalf of ARCHITECTURAL RECORD. *Prof. Labatut's acquaintance with Corbusier and his work dates from 1920*

CHAPEL

COVENTRY

A CONTEMPORARY EXPRESSION
OF CATHEDRAL TRADITIONS

A RARE ASSIGNMENT TODAY, *the design of a cathedral poses some problems for contemporary architecture. This design for the new Coventry Cathedral, to replace the one bombed out, represents a thoughtful effort to develop, in modern materials and methods, the traditional thinking on church concepts and inspirational necessities. It was chosen from 219 schemes in competition. On the following pages the architect relates his reasoning.* — Ed.

A CONTEMPORARY EXPRESSION OF CATHEDRAL TRADITIONS

By Basil Spence, O.B.E., A.R.A., A.R.S.A.

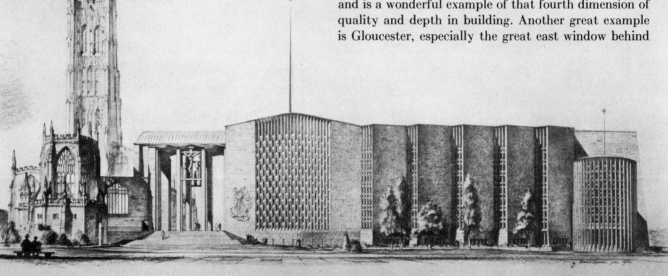

WHY did you design a "modernistic" cathedral when there were so many wonderful examples of pure gothic architecture in England which could be your model, giving perfect opportunities for a detailed copy? This question has often been put to me.

The answer is simply that I have studied these ancient cathedrals very carefully, being a Pugin student, for knowledge of Gothic was absolutely necessary before the prize could be awarded; and what I have tried to do is to apply what I thought to be the underlying principles of our own native architecture here in Britain.

Gothic architecture displays certain qualities, perhaps the most arresting of which is that their buildings were always modern when they were built, displaying a strong faith in their time, invention and courage. Things were done sometimes without adequate knowledge, with the result that spires and even vaults have fallen down. It is this spirit of inventiveness and faith in your own time, plus the great respect for the temple form, as this developed through the ages in the church of England, that dominated my approach to the rebuilding of Coventry Cathedral.

Some past examples are interesting. Durham, for instance, built eight hundred years ago as a modern building, strong, clear cut. The massing shows no hesitation whatever. This building has great vitality and poise, vitality that is felt to this day. Moreover it has the quality of looking as well in the rain as in the sun, and is a wonderful example of that fourth dimension of quality and depth in building. Another great example is Gloucester, especially the great east window behind the altar and the choir. Built in the middle of the fourteenth century and replacing a Norman choir, it showed the wisdom of the ecclesiastical authorities in encouraging the latest methods of design and construction, as the Romanesque architecture which it replaced was mostly wall and little window, whereas now this beautiful cathedral has a great east window 70 feet high and 40 feet across.

But England alone does not hold all the examples. An architect must throw his net wide. Let us look at

Pisa with the four elements, the basilica, the baptistry, the campanile and the campo santo, placed together with Grecian clarity and exactness, buildings that group in the third dimension and possess the fourth, quality.

At Ravenna, too, there are buildings which inspired me greatly; St. Apollinare in Classe, which is just outside Ravenna, built many hundreds of years ago as an early Christian basilica. This has for its massing a simple dignity of immaculate proportion and fenestration. The elements are all clearly defined, but externally it does not say much. It is a dignified building with an invitation to enter. It is the interior which matters, for here is the altar and it is here where men worship. The altar is enshrined in the most beautiful and dignified material, culminating in the apse, which is one of the most lovely mosaics I have ever seen, still a blaze of colour and as brilliant today as it ever was. The interior is rich with marbles and is flooded with a soft golden light through the alabaster windows. This building truly functions. Entering, the great surprise sweeps the

Also Ravenna (left) — "the altar is enshrined in the most beautiful and dignified materials"; and Albi for its impressive grandeur

visitor off his feet and turns him from a common visitor into a worshipper. It is this philosophy of design which had a strong bearing on the line I took in the rebuilding of Coventry Cathedral.

Very similar also is the effect at Albi in the south of France, a romantic town dominated by the cathedral, which is on the highest ground, standing there like a great hen with little chicks around her. But when you walk up to the cliff-like walls there is an impressive grandeur about the exterior, which is perhaps lacking in many other examples; it is severe and very dignified. It is only when one enters that the real magnificence of this building is appreciated. The philosophy is the same as that at Ravenna.

When I received my conditions for the rebuilding of Coventry, while I was in Edinburgh, I read them and was tremendously stimulated. I would like to quote the preface written by the Bishop and the Provost.

"The Cathedral is to speak to us and to generations to come of the Majesty, the Eternity and the Glory of God. God, therefore, direct you.

"It is a Cathedral of the Church of England. In terms of function, what should such a Cathedral express? It stands as a witness to the central dogmatic truths of the Christian Faith. Architecturally it should seize on those truths and thrust them upon the man who comes in from the street.

"The doctrine and the worship of the Church of England is liturgically centred in the Eucharist. The Cathedral should be built to enshrine the altar. This should be the ideal of the architect, not to conceive a building and to place in it an altar, but to conceive an altar and to create a building.

"In the Anglican liturgy it is the people's altar; the altar should gather the people, it should offer access for worship and invitation to Communion.

"With the altar — in the unity of worship — there is the preaching of the Gospel among our people of Coventry and the interpretation of the Word.

"The theology of the Cathedral we put before you to direct your thought. Prayer will be with you from the Cathedral Crypt and from the Diocese of Coventry. May God be with you in this great matter."

I determined at once to visit the site and see for myself. This Cathedral, as we all know, was bombed during the first of the great German air raids on Britain. It was destroyed by fire bombs on November 14th, 1940. There was great loss of life and property, but when I set foot in these ruins I realized I was walking on hallowed ground. Instead of the beautiful six hundred-year-old roof, this cathedral, because a cathedral it still is, has the skies as a vault. This feeling of reverence was intensified when I walked up to the altar which was erected during the war by a stone mason, from the stones which had fallen from the upper parts of the cathedral. Behind it is the charred cross made of beams that had not quite burnt out. This is an eloquent symbol, and a relic of faith during Britain's darkest hour, and I must admit to feelings of deep emotion when I saw this and read the words carved behind — "Father forgive."

I went to the site and looked out through the ruined windows over the ground reserved for the cathedral, and in a flash I saw in my mind's eye a beautiful new one growing out of the old, keeping the ruins as an integral part of the whole scheme. The picture I saw was a sparkling and beautiful altar at the end of a long vista backed by a great picture, the body of the nave spread out in front of the altar, but I did not see it clearly because in front of my eyes floated the bodies of the saints and the martyrs and it was through their bodies that the altar could be seen. We all know the price of this new altar — 1200 people killed and many, many more maimed and injured for life, 5,000 homes wiped out even with the people in them, 60,000 homes damaged, apart from the tremendous industrial damage. So the new altar will be seen through the saints and martyrs.

I took back with me to Edinburgh this idea seed, which continued to grow from that moment. Part of the new accommodation required is a chapel of unity where all church denominations could worship. This is a won-

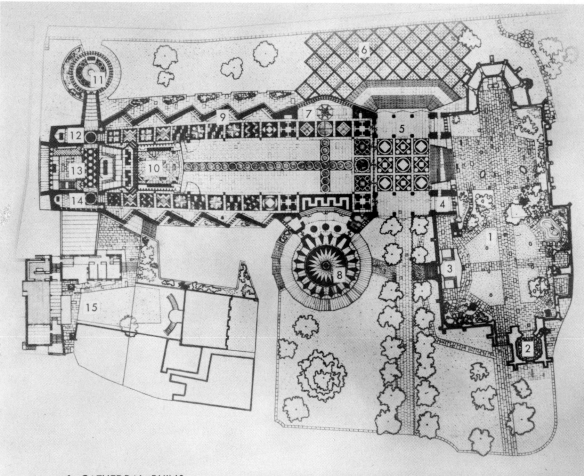

1 CATHEDRAL RUINS

2 TOWER

3 OPEN AIR STAGE

4 CRYPT CHAPEL ENTRANCES

5 ENTRANCE PORCH

6 FORECOURT

7 FONT

8 CHAPEL OF UNITY

9 HALLOWING PLACES

10 CHANCEL

11 GUILD CHAPEL AND CHAPTER HOUSE

12 CHAPEL OF THE RESURRECTION

13 LADY CHAPEL

14 CHILDREN'S CHAPEL

15 CHRISTIAN SERVICE CENTER

derful idea, worthy of strong architectural expression. I felt that this chapel could express unity and strength, and looking for a symbol to express it, I chose the star — a great star which will form a pattern on the floor, as the Star of Bethlehem was the first sign of Christian unity.

So opposite this chapel inside the new cathedral is the font. Because the font represents birth and virility and the rebirth of this cathedral, it is a very important feature. The font has a cover, a tall spire-shaped form, which rises to 80 feet. Behind it is a great window of 198 little windows. In each of these, I hope to have stained glass designs representing the saints in infancy, and the window will be carried out in the clear pure colours of birth and innocence.

People entering the cathedral first will see no other windows apart from this one, but their eyes should be drawn toward the altar, and beyond it to a great tapestry over 80 feet high and over 40 feet across. On this, in brilliant colours will be woven the figure of Our Lord seated in the glory of the Father with the four beasts, exactly as Saint John the Divine describes in his vision of the fourth chapter, Book of the Revelation. The designer of the tapestry is Graham Sutherland.

From Coventry Mr. Spence found inspiration in the simple altar built by a stone mason in the ruins of the cathedral, "a relic of faith during Britain's darkest hour," and from the ruins themselves, which he insisted be preserved as an integral part of the scheme for the new church

"... I saw in my mind's eye a beautiful new one growing out of the old ... a sparkling and beautiful altar at the end of a long vista ... but I did not see it clearly because in front of my eyes floated the bodies of the saints ..."

As you walk toward the altar you will realize that the windows reveal themselves as you reach them, because they are blotted from view by cliffs of stone, and you will only see them as you pass them.

There are five pairs of windows 70 feet high on opposite sides of the nave, each pair representing an age of man. The first pair grow from our birth — and represent childhood. These are strong virile windows in stained glass, strongly patterned. The colour is predominantly green and other colours allied to green, such as yellow and blue. These will present the young shoots growing out from the ground to the full height.

The next pair shows childhood growing into manhood and womanhood, the age of passion and strength, and these windows are predominantly red.

The next are the middle life with the experiences of middle life represented by the colours of the rainbow, some dark, some light, some brilliant and some dull.

Still going toward the altar, the next pair represent the richness and wisdom of old age and are deep blue and purple, flecked with gold.

You will notice that the windows are gradually becoming darker and richer as you move toward the altar; the last pair represent the after-life. These are the altar windows of golden glass. The light from these windows shines directly on to the altar, so as you approach the holy table there will always be this aura of golden light around it. But when you reach the altar and turn around, for the first time you will see all the windows at once. I do not know of a church so far built that does this. As you know life, you experience the present and can look back into the past, but you cannot see the future. But when you reach the altar, the whole pattern is revealed for the first time.

The two ranges of windows leading up to this climax represent on the right, the perfect side which is God, and on the left, the "man" side, a reflection of the perfect side but imperfect in its reflection, as man is always striving for perfection — rather like trees reflected in a pool disturbed by the wind. One is the truth and the other is rather an uncertain reflection of the truth. But at the altar both are joined in a blaze of glory.

As an instance of this, the wisdom window on the man side represents a great and beautiful chalice as the most beautiful thing a man can make in his wisdom. This is a strikingly rich window showing this chalice studded with jewels and brilliant in purple, blue and gold. But on the God side, the window represents the lily of perfection as the miracle of planting a seed. Something so perfect as a lily growing cannot be imitated and even under a microscope the lily is still perfect.

A cathedral in England has a greater purpose than a church in which only to hold services. The Cathedral will open every day and must speak all the time, even when there is no sermon to be heard or anthem to be listened to. It must speak itself. The object of this cathedral is to turn the visitor who may go into the cathedral alone for a half hour's peace — to turn him from a visitor into a worshipper.

The vault will be a free standing structure within the building, of concrete on 14 steel columns or legs resting on crystal balls. The author mentions in his notes the inspirational quality of the vault in King's College Chapel, Cambridge (shown at left)

THE CHURCH AND ITS SCHOOL

4

By C. Harry Atkinson, Editor, **Protestant Churches: administration and equipment;** *Associate Editor,* **Christian Herald.**

COMPARISON of a present day church building with that of yesterday reveals some striking changes. Adult worship once claimed practically all of every church building dollar. Today, a seven-day-a-week program of purposeful activities for all ages demands facilities running all the way from the babyfold and crib to craft rooms for elder citizens.

Planning for education

Fifty cents of practically every church building dollar are now expended for educational purposes and for a variety of indoor and outdoor recreational and fellowship facilities. A present day church, when planning educational facilities, is giving far greater attention to the details. Rooms are being related definitely to the capacities and interests of each age group; are being planned in relation to each other, with a view to better administration and greater flexibility of use and space. Far more attention is being given to the philosophy of education and to the psychology of the pupils than heretofore, and as a result, the buildings are much more intimately related to the needs and interests of growing and developing persons.

Four basic questions

The questions which the modern church school planner asks of the church school building are these:

Is it healthy, and safe, and comfortable?

Is it designed to further the learning program of children and adults?

Is the space so designed, and is the building so constructed as to permit greater flexibility in the use, and in the greater variety of activities so the educational pattern and the grouping of the children are not frozen?

More particularly, is the teaching space in which children live and work while within the church attractive?

Search for the spiritual

These questions indicate that today's church buildings must be planned from the inside out and must be geared to human requirements; physical, psychological and spiritual. The complicated structure which makes up the modern church is beginning to show a new honesty, efficiency, and esthetic quality by which tangible expression is given of the functions of the church in modern materials and by means of modern methods of construction. The better work today carries with it intimations of the long spiritual heritage of the Christian Church.

Church School conference

A recent three-day conference brought together for the first time architects from various sections of the country, nationally recognized religious educational specialists for each of the age level groups, and the church building executives of the churches comprising the Bureau of Church Building of the National Council of Churches. During this significant conference, certain standards for educational space and equipment for today's church edifice were arrived at. The following statement of the recommended requirements is a far cry from what was acceptable a few years ago.

Creative teaching

Foremost in the thinking of this conference was a concept that teaching is a much more varied, democratic, and creative undertaking than that of imparting information to children and youth while seated about a table in a cramped classroom. Emphasis was placed upon ample space, especially for small children to permit greater freedom of movement, a variety of purposeful activities, and the avoidance of over-crowding — so detrimental to the physical and psychological well-being of children.

The following norm of standards were adopted both as to maximum pupil load per room, square footage of floor space per pupil, and as to general characteristics of spaces within the buildings.

Requirements for Children

Under three years

The basic consideration for this age group was: how can the church best serve the family unit, both parents and children during their infancy and earliest years. Where the church assumes responsibility for children of two years and younger, the following standards should be strictly adhered to:

Floor surfaces should be easily cleaned and warm enough for small children to sit or play on them comfortably.

There should be a separate place for each 12 infants (not walking) or for eight toddlers. Separate rooms are desirable; separate space enclosed by dividers will serve.

There should be space to permit 3 ft between cribs for infants; toddlers should have at least 30 sq ft per child.

Toddlers should be provided with child's size toilet facilities, and a child's height wash basin for each eight pupils.

The size of the tables should be restricted to 24 in. by 30 in. by 18 in. in height for the nursery children, slightly higher for the kindergarten and primary departments.

Adjoining facilities should provide for heating and storing such food as may be required for small children.

While parents should not be permitted in the small children's rooms in the interest of sanitation, these rooms should be adjacent to and accessible to a reception area. It is recommended that a small room should be provided where a leader can take a small child who has become upset or ill to await the arrival of his parents in relative quiet.

It is important that a direct entrance from outside should be provided for the section of the building assigned to preschool children.

Windows should be of clear glass, and low — 24 to 30 in. above the floor in the nursery and kindergarten departments. It is not necessary to provide room for group activities other than those areas mentioned for children under three years of age.

Three year olds

Here 35 sq ft per pupil is rated good. This permits space for moving about freely among the interest centers within the room which is so necessary for effective teaching of children of this age. Twenty-five to 30 sq ft per pupil is rated fair; under 25 sq ft per pupil, poor.

It is recommended that not more than 15 children of this age should be in one classroom. Fifteen to 18 pupils is rated fair. More than 18 pupils, poor. Overcrowding often frightens small children who need individual attention.

Four and five year olds

The same general standards recommended for three year old children obtain for children four and five years of age. No room for children of this age should be smaller than 15 ft by 20 ft, even if this makes necessary a temporary combination of two age groups within a given room. Dimension here is critical.

Rooms should generally be rectangular in shape with proportions of 3 to 4 — or 4 to 5. Wherever possible, the long dimension of each room should be on the outside wall to permit large window area. One wall should provide display space. Twenty pupils of this age group in a single room is rated good; 20 to 25 pupils fair; over 25 pupils poor.

Once children have attained elementary school age the church school pupil load is increased per room, and the square footage per pupil is slightly reduced.

Thirty to 35 sq ft per pupil is rated good; 25 to 30 sq ft fair; under 25 sq ft poor.

Six to twelve year olds

Children in the grades of public school can be handled successfully in groups as large as 30.

Emphasis is placed upon the need to provide adequate storage space for every room.

There is a strong tendency away from the formal worship centers in the preschool and elementary children's classrooms. Today, all activities are carried on in a single room.

Requirements for Young People

Quite understandably the churches are spending a large share of their educational, recreational and social dollars on the age group 12 to 18; the junior and senior high school range. Appeal to these young people must be most carefully made in this stage of their development when steadying directions are difficult to achieve and maintain.

Provisions for youth activities in terms of space, equipment and particularly the character of the space are most critical matters. Here careful planning and good designs can often make the difference between maintaining the participation and enthusiasm of youth or losing them to completely outside interests.

Loads and spaces

In the junior high and high school divisions, the recommended pupil load is 20 for junior high pupils and 25 for the senior high and older youth. Fifteen to 18 sq ft per pupil is considered good; 12 to 15 sq ft fair; and 10 to 12 sq ft poor. Here again, the provision of adequate floor space is deemed important to permit a greater variety of teaching procedures and a sense of freedom and livable conditions within a given room.

In some instances, pupils of this age will be provided with one room large enough to assemble the whole age group for such activities as they need to carry on as a unit. If this procedure is followed, there should be classrooms adjacent of the sizes mentioned where the classroom and more intimate study work can be carried on in smaller groups.

Extracurricular activities

In many instances, these larger assembly rooms serve many purposes, and are often equipped with a small kitchenette which provides opportunity for sociable affairs and refreshments.

It is recommended that churches plan these rooms with a view not only to meeting the church school requirements, but also the extracurricular activities of young people.

In larger churches, snack bars and a rendezvous room where youth may gather for sociability under supervision, are much in evidence. Religious leaders find that young people will often discuss serious religious problems in these informal occasions, with the record player or television or radio going full blast. In fact, the informal gathering of people together within a church building is more and more becoming an important approach to a natural discussion of religious and personal problems.

Equipment and furnishings

It is recommended that no matter what the numerical size of a class of young people is, the room should never be less than 12 ft by 15 ft in square footage. Here again, the whole concept of multiple use and flexibility of use is emphasized.

In youth departments, sturdy folding chairs which provide comfortable seating make possible a flexible arrangement and multiple use of space and equipment.

Chalk boards, maps of the roller type, plenty of cabinets for storing material, and carefully selected pictures with an appeal for youth are standard equipment for their rooms.

Reading and recreation

Where the church budget will permit, a youth lounge with a fireplace is highly recommended for after church get-togethers and for discussion groups so much enjoyed by youth. Increasingly, a good church library with youth reference library is being installed in the modern church. Craft and game rooms in basement areas are important. The many clubs, Scout units, and other organizations of the church find increasing use for this kind of creative group activity.

While the trend is definitely away from gymnasiums and spaces for heavy athletic events, greater emphasis is being placed upon providing plenty of rooms of various sizes for the informal social gathering of small groups.

Requirements for Adults

Loads and spaces

The increasing number of elder citizens being added to our population each year, some 400,000 of them, presents a new challenge to the church to provide space, equipment, and opportunity for these older people to enjoy each other's company and to engage in creative activities suitable to their ages.

While youth can readily make use of the upper floors and buildings where it is necessary because of limited land use to erect such structures, adults should preferably be on floors which are close to grade and easily approached.

There is a noticeable tendency away from the very large adult classes running into memberships and attendance of 100 or more. Attempts are being made to organize adult work on the basis of interest groups and to keep the size of the groups to such numbers as will permit a more intimate friendship and a more general participation of the class in discussion.

Adult classrooms should be computed on the basis of 10 sq ft of floor space per pupil. This means that a class of 40 members will need approximately 400 sq ft of floor space or a room approximately 16 ft by 24 ft. For the reasons mentioned above, it is hoped that adult classes will not exceed from 40 to 50 members at the most.

Seating arrangements

While adults usually are accustomed to sitting in formally arranged seatings, the tendency today is to make the adult classroom far less formal. Additional floor space and the careful selection of furniture permit a more homelike atmosphere in the adult classroom and the arrangement of seating in such a way as to give a sense of group participation rather than the lecture method of teaching.

A small kitchenette adjacent to adult classrooms makes it possible to use these rooms for small social occasions and for club or group meetings. In the design of this, flexibility of arrangement for maximum use is difficult but completely necessary for efficient use of the space.

Recreational requirements

As with youth, craft activities are becoming increasingly popular among adults, and frequently create great interest in games or other forms of physical recreation. Men and women enjoy learning new skills or improving upon old ones, and in creating things which are both useful and beautiful. These classrooms can be equipped as elaborately as the interests of the adults demand, and as can be carried by the funds available. In some instances, ceramic kilns, power saws, knitting paraphernalia, sewing machines, leather tooling equipment, carpenter tools, and other related equipment are made available.

Dining provisions

At least one large room should be arranged for the large banquets or dinners which should characterize the program of the modern church and for special dramatic or audio-visual programs as may from time to time be presented by the church. Here again, emphasis needs to be placed upon the fact that the new methods of lighting, heating and ventilating, and the new fabrics with which even an old building can be refurbished, make it unnecessary for any church to have a gloomy, unhealthy building, either from the standpoint of the room areas or the toilet facilities or the corridors and entrances.

Kitchen requirements

From 10 to 12 sq ft per person is the requirement for a large dining or banquet hall. Kitchen facilities, which should be immediately adjacent, will require extra space. In the modern church, it is important that the kitchen be well planned by a competent architect or kitchen engineer, and that the many pieces of equipment which ease the labor of volunteer workers, should be installed. Today this equipment is available in price ranges suitable to the building budget of every church; the determination of equipment needs for kitchen, class and craft rooms should be among the very first acts of the architect as he begins the design of these facilities.

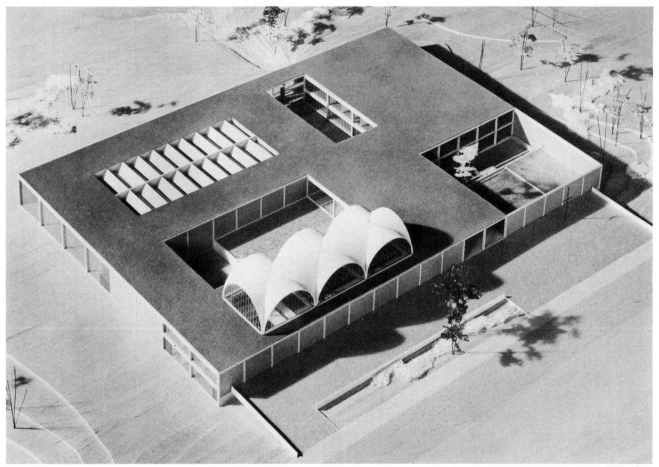

Howard Studio

* GRACE LUTHERAN CHURCH, TEANECK, N. J.

Paul Schweikher, Architect

* Premiated in the 1955 Awards Program of the Church Architectural Guild of America

IN THIS PROJECTED BUILDING, all of the problems normally attendant upon the integration of adjunct facilities with the sanctuary are not only present, but particularly insistent because of the necessity of providing for a fully-equipped parochial school plant. Here skillful handling of the courtyard is the great unifying device. An increasing number of architects are finding the use of the courtyard effective in church planning as well as in other building types. Proper organization of such sequestered outdoor rooms affords multiple values for all who use the church. As intermediate spaces arranged to prepare those entering the sanctuary from the street, their role is significant.

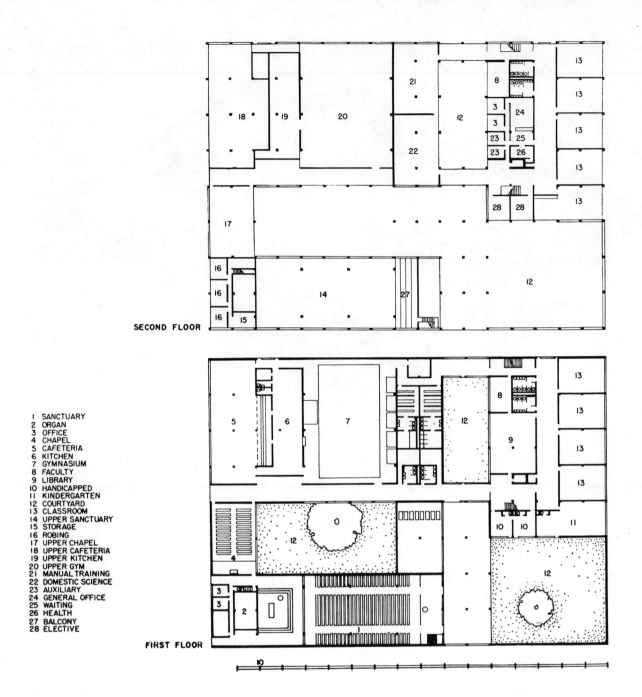

SECOND FLOOR

1 SANCTUARY
2 ORGAN
3 OFFICE
4 CHAPEL
5 CAFETERIA
6 KITCHEN
7 GYMNASIUM
8 FACULTY
9 LIBRARY
10 HANDICAPPED
11 KINDERGARTEN
12 COURTYARD
13 CLASSROOM
14 UPPER SANCTUARY
15 STORAGE
16 ROBING
17 UPPER CHAPEL
18 UPPER CAFETERIA
19 UPPER KITCHEN
20 UPPER GYM
21 MANUAL TRAINING
22 DOMESTIC SCIENCE
23 AUXILIARY
24 GENERAL OFFICE
25 WAITING
26 HEALTH
27 BALCONY
28 ELECTIVE

FIRST FLOOR

In furnishing informal gathering spaces after services, they serve a time-honored and highly desirable activity. The spatial sensations and the resultant emotional situations that can be experienced in the juxtaposition of indoor and outdoor rooms, are particularly appealing in a building which to a degree must compete with secular attractions. Finally, there is a powerful appeal to the intellect for both architect and church member in the recognition that in the courtyard there is an expression of a long tradition in buildings generally, and churches particularly.

The grouping of all the elements within an enclosing wall and the use of the groin vault forms, further emphasize a strong link with an historical tradition.

Grace Lutheran's Senior Pastor, Rev. Theodore W. Beiderwieden, reports that though unusual, the proposal has excited real enthusiasm in the congregation and among denominational leaders.

Construction on the seven-acre site will begin with the educational unit which is planned for 300 children with two special sections for the handicapped, whose difficulty with stairs dictated ramp circulation throughout the building. This special requirement made still more difficult the architect's job of achieving unity.

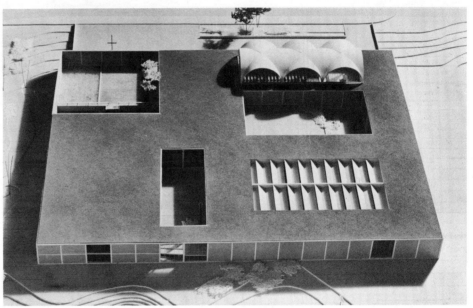

Howard Studio

FROM THE ARCHITECT: Mr. Earl P. Carlin of Schweikher's office reports: The structural system is to be an exposed concrete frame with curtain walls of masonry, glass or metal panels between columns.

One of Mr. Schweikher's purposes was to create a separate environment within the walls, not unlike the feeling of medieval monastic cloisters, hence the courtyards providing interior vistas. An additional advantage of this plan makes it possible, for reasons of economics, to build the structure in sections, with each unit complete within itself, eliminating the usual amputated look of partly finished construction work.

Cost (Estimated): $1,000,000
Area: 52,000 sq ft

141

* CHAPELWOOD METHODIST CHURCH, HOUSTON

Hamilton Brown, Architect
Scheider Construction Co., General Contractor

* Premiated in the 1955 Awards Program of the Church Architectural Guild of America

THIS CHURCH is designed to seat 500; to furnish educational, social and recreational facilities for 200 at present, 500 ultimately; and to include a chapel for 100.

The sanctuary building and one-third of the classroom facilities have been constructed. Eventual plan includes two more of the courtyard centered classroom wings with covered passageways surrounding three sides of each court and interconnecting from court to court.

Particularly noteworthy is the fitness of the open courtyard units for a growing church where the budget permits building only one unit at a time. The overhangs of porch and passageways particularly suit the climate.

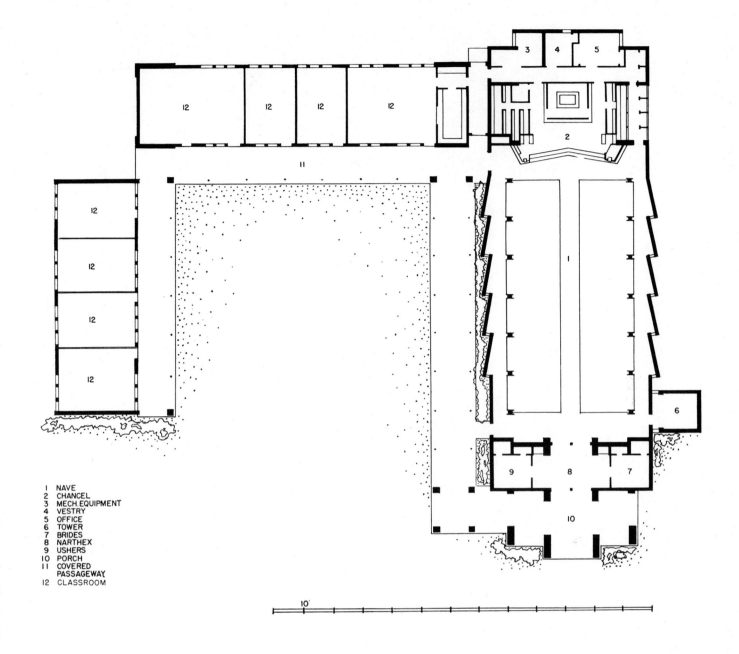

1 NAVE
2 CHANCEL
3 MECH.EQUIPMENT
4 VESTRY
5 OFFICE
6 TOWER
7 BRIDES
8 NARTHEX
9 USHERS
10 PORCH
11 COVERED
    PASSAGEWAY
12 CLASSROOM

10'

FROM THE ARCHITECT: This church serves a group of middle-income, young-to-middle-age people living an informal life in an attractive wooded area on the outskirts of the city of Houston.

Foremost in the mind of the architect was the thought that the environment created by the architecture must be closely related to the character of this particular congregation, as well as the form and content of the worship service desired by the congregation.

Emphasis is placed on the altar area of the chancel as the significant aspect of the worship service. Exterior light sources directed toward the altar area are arranged so that the original source of light is not visible to the congregation when facing the altar. Interior lighting for night services has been designed to function in a similar manner.

The materials employed in the construction of the building are in the main used in their natural finish and lend, with their warmth, a character of informality.

The use of music has played an important part in the design of the building. Dramatic use of the choir may be employed through opening the ambulatory to the upper chancel sides and narthex to the upper nave, thus permitting processional music to carry into the sanctuary before the choir's entry.

143

F. W. Seiders

Nave framing is carried out with steel bents. Framing in the classroom wings uses wood trusses. Exterior walls of the church proper are of solid masonry; those of the classroom wings are brick veneer on wood frame. Interior walls of the church are handmade Mexican brick on the nave sides; perforated hardboard acoustical tile at the rear; and fabric-backed redwood staves at the rear of the chancel. Classroom interior walls are plywood. The roof is 4 in. tongue and groove cedar planking, built-up, gravel topped. Floor is cork tile in the nave; carpeting in chancel. Communion rail is in white birch.

Cost: $187,174.62 (including pews and chancel furnishings; excluding land, landscaping, furniture and fees)
Area: 16,418 sq ft

* CHURCH OF THE NATIVITY, HONOLULU, T. H.

Law & Wilson, Architects and Engineers
James J. Oberhausen, Electrical Engineer
Eugene Urbain, Mechanical Engineer
Harold Tanimura, Site Engineer
E. D. Phillips, Designer
Robert V. Davis, Furniture Designer
Richard R. Hadano, Contractor

* Premiated in the 1955 Awards Program of the Church Architectural Guild of America

THIS EPISCOPAL CHURCH provides seating for 380 in the sanctuary, 20 in the choir and 90 in a children's chapel. In addition, provision has been made for a Sunday school incorporating a day school for 160 pupils.

The organization of these facilities around the deep forecourt particularly urged bringing this building to the attention of architects who will recognize in the application of the ancient "atrium" element a rich source of appeal to the senses and the minds of those people who pass through it on their way to worship.

The walled courtyards on either side of the nave shut out the distractions of a nearby highway and complete the cloistered theme.

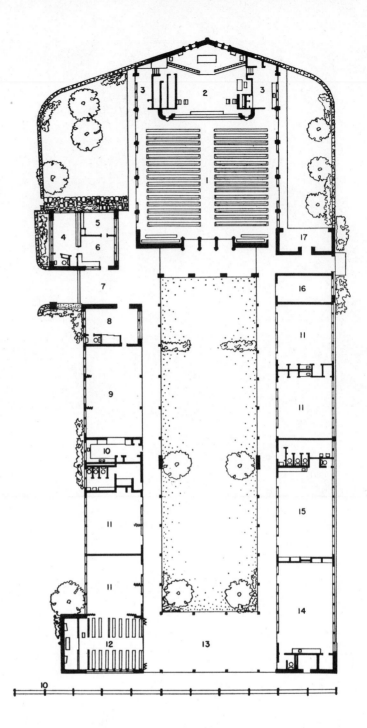

1 NAVE
2 CHANCEL
3 SACRISTY
4 VICAR'S OFFICE
5 ASS'T VICAR
6 SECRETARY
7 MAIN ENTRY
8 CHOIR PRACTICE
9 MEETING ROOMS
10 KITCHEN
11 CLASSROOM
12 CHILDREN'S CHAPEL
13 LANAI
14 NURSERY
15 KINDERGARTEN
16 STORAGE
17 COLUMBARIUM

FROM THE ARCHITECT: The first small congregation of the Church of the Nativity had been meeting in a barn belonging to a local dairy, and it was perhaps this humble setting which led them to name their completed church after the Nativity of Christ.

In a four-stage operation, completely equipped day school rooms were built first, followed by partly completed Sunday school rooms and the children's chapel. This chapel served as the church for nearly three years. The day school had grown so that two classrooms were added, and last year the church was completed.

Much thought was given to ensuring that the church should not be foreign to the land, that it should rise naturally from the soil and from the needs of its people. It is built of lava field stone gathered from neighboring hills. The pews, altar furniture, and panelling are made from the beautiful Hawaiian "koa" wood.

The distinguishing aspect of this church, aside from its adaptability to the Hawaiian scene, is its warm, family atmosphere. It was deliberately designed to draw children and parents together in their worship. The function of the courtyard in achieving this goal will be apparent. It is an integrating element of the strongest sort.

Williams

Nave framing is laminated fir trusses. Exterior walls are of volcanic field stone gathered nearby. Interior walls are paneled in koa wood. The roof consists of 2 in. redwood sheathing covered with cedar shakes. Louvers are in redwood and glass jalousies are employed in the openings. Mullions, exterior cross, pulpit, lectern and altar rail are in cast stone. The lanaii uses a coral aggregate simulating travertine. Pews are in koa wood. Altar and cross are in green marble.

Cost: $196,533
Area: 15,806 sq ft

BETH ISRAEL SYNAGOGUE AND SCHOOL, OMAHA

Kivett and Myers, Architects
Angus McCallum, Associate
Steele, Sandham and Steele, Supervising Architects
Pfuhl and Shideler, Structural Engineers
W. L. Cassell, Mechanical Engineer
Cooper Construction Co., General Contractor
Miller Electric Co., Electrical Contractor
Natkin Engineering Co., Plumbing and Heating Contractor

PARTIALLY COMPLETED in 1953, and awarded the medal of the Kansas City Chapter of the A.I.A., this building seats over 650 in the sanctuary and an additional 800 in the congregational assembly hall which seats 400 at dining tables.

Here again is seen the use of the courtyard as an integral element in the design. Principal entrances to it may be made from either the driveway approach or from the main corridor which separates the assembly hall from the religious education unit.

The carefully organized plan provides for the great variety of use demanded by all religious buildings today.

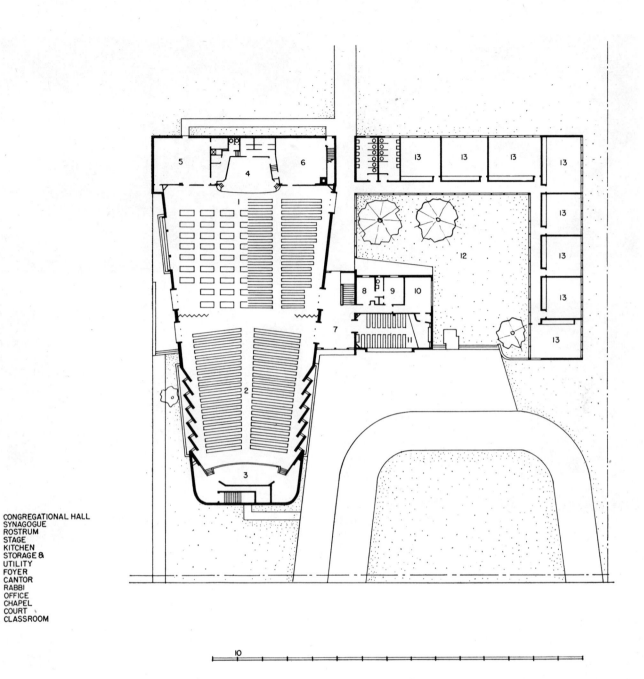

1 CONGREGATIONAL HALL
2 SYNAGOGUE
3 ROSTRUM
4 STAGE
5 KITCHEN
6 STORAGE &
  UTILITY
7 FOYER
8 CANTOR
9 RABBI
10 OFFICE
11 CHAPEL
12 COURT
13 CLASSROOM

FROM THE ARCHITECT: Herewith some interpretation of the various symbols used in the Sanctuary: at the front of the auditorium, the two high walls on either side of the Ark covered with Stars of David, worked out in a three dimension pattern on a walnut background, are symbolic of the two tablets of the Ten Commandments, which are in turn joined, and partially covered by, a central curtain indicative of the curtain covering the Holy of Holies in the Temple. The curtain is golden, symbolic of the magnificent curtain that covered the Ark in the days of the Temple. Above the Ark is the high Menorah with seven branches, just as there was one in the ancient days; it is symbolic of the creation of light and to the left is the Eternal Light, eternally reminding of the light that never failed in the Temple. One approaches the Ark by going up five stairs, these are symbolic of the five books of Moses; and the twelve windows and jutting walls are, of course, representative of the twelve tribes of Israel.

In Contemporary Jewish Houses of Worship a great effort is being made to make them uniquely American in form and spirit, and to establish a conscious and creative synagogue for our country. Architects will recognize that the design problems in synagogues today are in many ways unique.

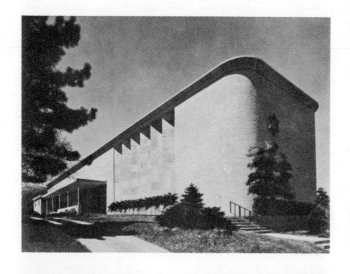

Foundations here are reinforced concrete. Framing is steel. Exterior walls are light buff face brick and Indiana limestone with shot sawn finish. Interior walls are plaster. Partitions are masonry block. Roof is steel deck. The ceiling combines plaster and mineral type acoustical tiles; kitchen — metal pans. Floors are asphalt tile and terrazzo. Windows are steel frame. Exterior door is aluminum. Folding door partition between sanctuary and social hall is one of the largest of such installations.

Cost: $418,000 (exclusive of religious school)
Area: 20,957 sq ft

*FIRST BAPTIST CHURCH, EVERETT, WASH.

Durham, Anderson and Freed, Architects

Premiated in the 1955 Awards Program of the Church Architectural Guild of America

WITH AN EXTREMELY SMALL downtown lot, and a very low per capita budget, the architects of this building faced an unusually difficult problem of planning.

On a lot 120 ft by 194 ft, they were asked to provide sanctuary seats for 800; religious education facilities, including adults, for 800 to 950; dining facilities for 400; and a chapel for 100 or more persons.

The use of an entrance forecourt and rear and side courts provides an increased amount of light and vista as well as the means of unifying the many complex elements demanded in a large city church with a wide-ranging program of varied activities.

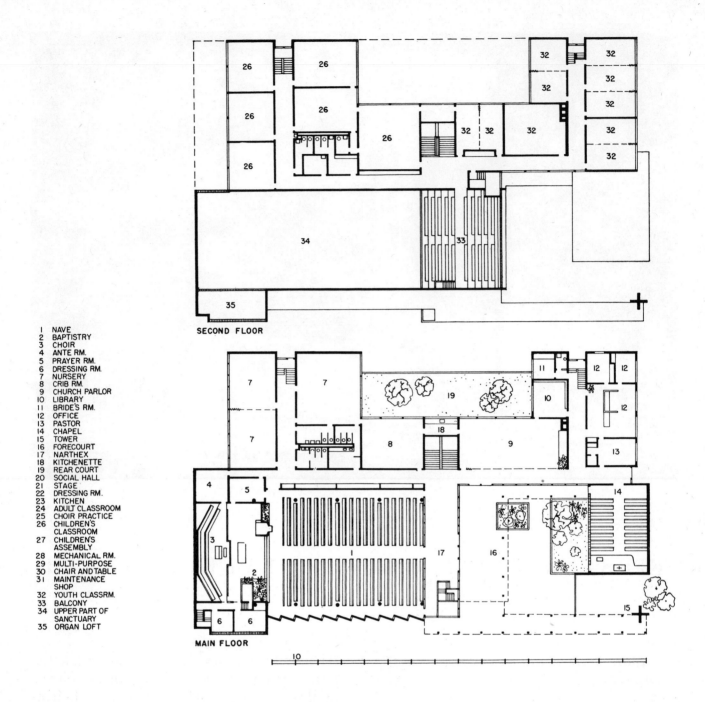

1 NAVE
2 BAPTISTRY
3 CHOIR
4 ANTE RM.
5 PRAYER RM.
6 DRESSING RM.
7 NURSERY
8 CRIB RM.
9 CHURCH PARLOR
10 LIBRARY
11 BRIDE'S RM.
12 OFFICE
13 PASTOR
14 CHAPEL
15 TOWER
16 FORECOURT
17 NARTHEX
18 KITCHENETTE
19 REAR COURT
20 SOCIAL HALL
21 STAGE
22 DRESSING RM.
23 KITCHEN
24 ADULT CLASSROOM
25 CHOIR PRACTICE
26 CHILDREN'S
   CLASSROOM
27 CHILDREN'S
   ASSEMBLY
28 MECHANICAL RM.
29 MULTI-PURPOSE
30 CHAIR AND TABLE
31 MAINTENANCE
   SHOP
32 YOUTH CLASSRM.
33 BALCONY
34 UPPER PART OF
   SANCTUARY
35 ORGAN LOFT

SECOND FLOOR

MAIN FLOOR

FROM THE ARCHITECT: The entrance to the church, chapel, and religious education spaces through the landscaped court creates, on a site lacking the appeal of a suburban tree-covered area, a composition pleasing in its relationship and interesting in its possibilities for texture, color and pattern.

Circulation on the main floor has been dramatized to connect the use of the chapel, church parlor and nave with the adjacent areas accommodating the administration offices and the space for the youngest children, in order that mothers will not have to leave this floor. The religious education space is organized into typical departmental areas. Large classrooms are grouped around assembly areas for group worship with the purpose of alternating the use of worship and study space by separate groups. This church is unique in its development of adult classes which form an unusual percentage of the Sunday School attendance. Classroom areas have been kept as large and flexible as possible, well-lighted, and integrated with vertical circulation.

A multi-purpose area on the basement level is a compromise to find space for active play to meet those who wish to emphasize gymnasium activities. The social hall will be designed for multiple use, but it is not intended for gymnasium activity.

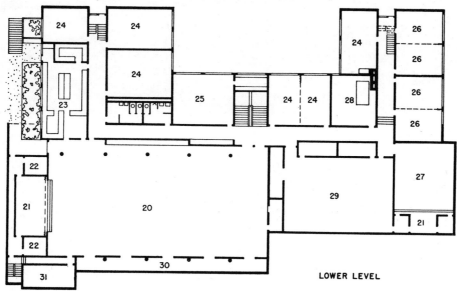

LOWER LEVEL

Construction will be carried out in reinforced concrete using prestressed beams and slabs. Exterior walls will be faced with native stone and will result in a combination of exposed concrete, stone and glass. Interior walls will be plastered with large areas of sound-absorbing plaster. Partitions will be 2 in. plaster and the ceiling will be suspended. Floors will be finished in asphalt tile. Aluminum sash will be used for windows. Plastic sky domes are proposed in the garden court to illuminate multi-purpose room below. The heating system will be oil-fired, hot water with zone control.

Cost (estimated): $563,000 (including furnishings, fees, sales tax)
Area: 42,603 sq ft

ST. PETER'S LUTHERAN CHURCH, NORWALK, CT.

Pedersen and Tilney, Architects

THE PROGRAM for this building made these five major demands: a minimum of 300 seats in the nave and a maximum educational and parish activity area for the use of somewhat over 300 children from the neighborhood; a church which would conform properly to the established liturgical pattern of this Lutheran denomination; careful use of the irregularly contoured three-acre site in its pleasant suburban environment; a modern building of simple materials but without experimental forms; and a building of minimum cost. The chairman of the building committee is a merchant builder. The success of the architects in meeting these demands is evident here.

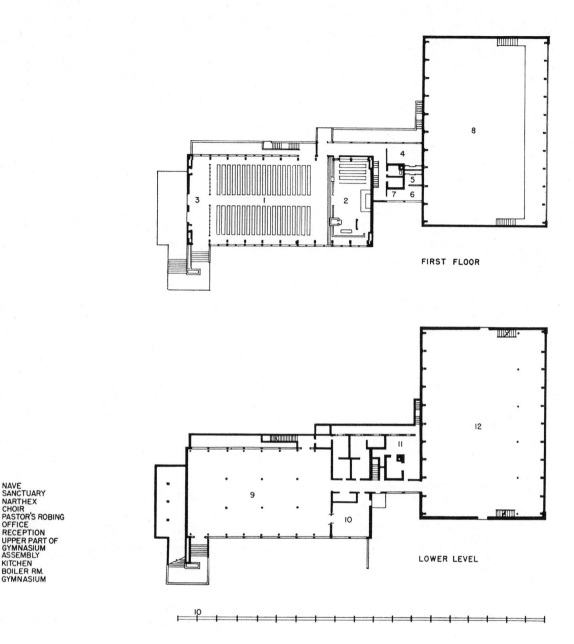

FIRST FLOOR

1 NAVE
2 SANCTUARY
3 NARTHEX
4 CHOIR
5 PASTOR'S ROBING
6 OFFICE
7 RECEPTION
8 UPPER PART OF
  GYMNASIUM
9 ASSEMBLY
10 KITCHEN
11 BOILER RM.
12 GYMNASIUM

LOWER LEVEL

FROM THE ARCHITECT: The new church for St. Peter's Lutheran Congregation is strongly in the contemporary style characterized by the simple straightforward use of everyday materials — brick, redwood, glass and concrete — organized so they create a structure having the dignity and character required by a Lutheran church.

Use has been made of the natural contours of the site so three divisions of the building, the church proper, the fellowship building with gymnasium and the assembly hall, all receive the maximum of natural light and ventilation and so these elements of the church create a pleasing and harmonious composition. A sim-

ple open bell tower dominates the center of the building group.

The new church will be equipped with special lighting complementing the dramatic glass walls but will otherwise be plainly furnished. It will be fully air conditioned and will be provided with facilities such as kitchens and locker rooms for social and athletic gatherings.

(Editor's note: It is interesting to note that in this example — one of two in this group which do not employ the courtyard as an element — the site is pleasantly wooded, interestingly contoured and relatively quiet; in light of this there is no need for the court device.)

Framing in this building employs laminated bents. Exterior walls of gymnasium and nave ends, originally intended to be in stone are presently proposed to be carried out in brick. Interior walls of the nave will be redwood siding. Roof will be 5-ply, built up, topped with white gravel. Floors in gymnasium will be hardwood; in the nave asphalt tile. Open tower will be in wood frame with poured concrete base. Narthex porch will be paved in flagstone. Narthex screen will be of plywood.

Cost (estimated): $250,000
Area: 21,500 sq ft

AN UNUSUAL DESIGN FOR COLLEGIATE RELIGION

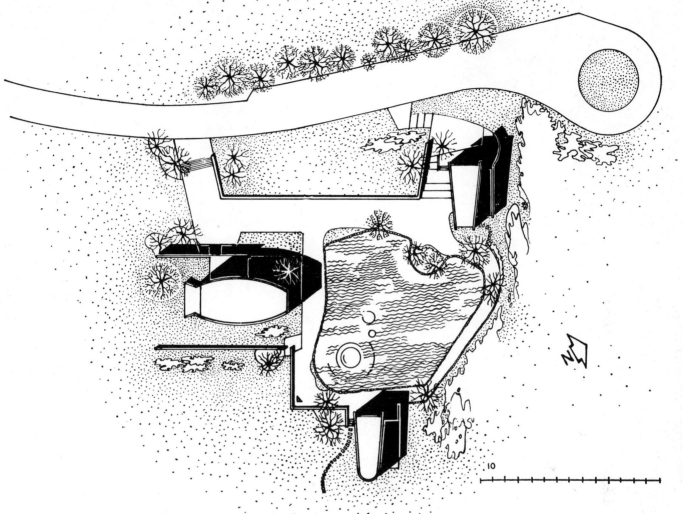

Drawings by Thad Leski of Harrison & Abramovitz

Interfaith Center, Brandeis University, Waltham, Mass.   *Harrison & Abramovitz, Architects*

Structural Engineers — *Eipel Engineering*; Mechanical & Electrical Engineers — *Sears & Kopf*; Utilities Engineers — *Linenthal & Becker*; Acoustical Engineers — *Bolt, Beranek & Newman*; Lighting Consultant — *Lighting by Feder*; General Contractor — *Lilly Construction Co.*; Interior Consultant — *Alice Tiebout*; Sculpture (Eternal Light & Menorah) — *Herbert Ferber*; Ark Curtain — *Design, Mitchell Siporin* — *Execution, Helen Kramer*; Ark, Lecterns, Furniture — *built by Jens Risom*; Religious Appointments *executed by Rambush*.

THREE CHAPELS: JEWISH

Architect Max Abramovitz says:

"Following the development of a program at Brandeis University to provide equal and distinct facilities for the Catholic, Protestant and Jewish faiths, it became apparent after many studies that the best solution would be three distinct structures — not one with subdivisions or movable appointments within. Each group would then have its own atmosphere and quality — possible only with special attention to individual space and concern for specific religious ritual and procedure. Thus developed the idea of three chapels grouped about a pond adjacent to a growth of trees. The composition permits a view of each building in relation to the other, as well as a vista from the campus proper.

"Although varied in shape and design — expressive of the peculiar characteristics and functions within — a feeling of unity and neighborliness was provided by

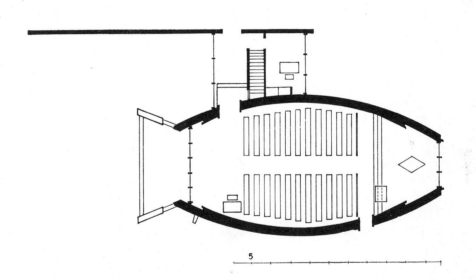

5

Max Abramovitz:

using similar materials and a like character throughout. Competition was avoided by an absence of exterior symbolism — yet individual identification becomes apparent to one strolling about the pond. There is the Ark form in the Jewish chapel; the Communion table in the Protestant chapel; the Altar for the Catholic chapel — all readily apparent through the plate glass and wood screens that open to the pond.

"The Catholic chapel is round-ended. The enclosed east end envelops the ritual of the high Mass and helps achieve a low lighting level; the open, glass-walled west end reveals the altar from without. The Protestant chapel is of bold trapezoidal shape with glass and white-oak end walls, the walls focusing on the Communion table and sky beyond. The Jewish chapel is formed of two solid curved screens of brick with end walls of oak

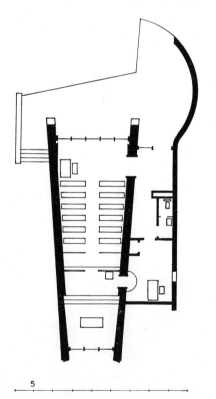

5

THREE CHAPELS: CATHOLIC

Max Abramovitz:

and glass, yielding a view through to the Ark and the grouped trees beyond.

"Architecturally, the aim was to develop a special atmosphere within the group which would set it apart from the academic buildings and develop an inner mood associated with today's three major faiths.

"The ceilings are visually separated from the walls for a floating effect, which is furthered by side-lighting for an impression of airiness. They also slope downwards toward Altar, Communion table or Ark to accent the focal points for each of the faiths. The floors are all of dark oak planking, and the end screens uniformly of natural finish white-oak and polished plate glass for exterior unity. Great care was taken in both the design and execution of the ritualistic furnishings, executed by leading artists."

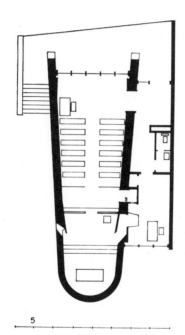

5

CHAPEL: INTERDENOMINATIONAL

Eero Saarinen and Associates, Architects

Anderson and Beckwith, Associate Architects

Ammann and Whitney, Structural Engineers

Hyde and Bobbis, Mechanical and Electrical Engineers

Bolt, Beranek & Newman, Acoustical Engineers

George A. Fuller Company, General Contractors

EERO SAARINEN was asked to design M.I.T.'s Kresge Chapel to serve the needs of Jewish, Roman Catholic and Protestant faiths. The hemmed-in site on the West Campus was almost as difficult as the program. The final building is a clear response to both.

The architect, in effect, was asked to resolve differences historically unresolvable in terms of architectural space and form. The resolution has been made in

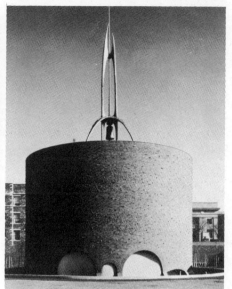

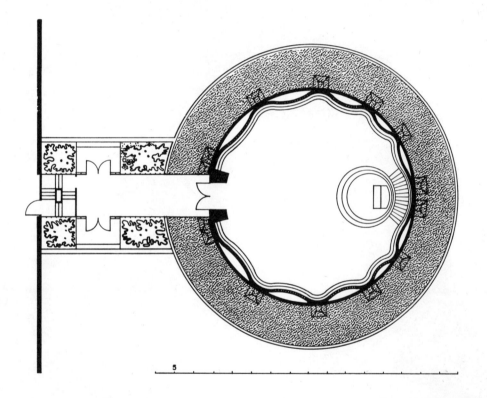

5

M. I. T. Chapel

terms of the least common denominator, and in this moated, windowless structure of simple shape, the high sense of removal and calm necessary to meditation has been achieved.

Natural light enters the chapel through a honeycombed baffled lantern and through a ribbon of horizontal wainscote glazing (see detail). Reflected upward from the water, this light plays on the brick surface of the inner wall which undulates irregularly to prevent acoustical focus. The shallow inverted cone of the suspended plaster ceiling and the brick grillwork of the lower walls are also in response to acoustic determinants.

The gilt metal screen behind the marble pedestal is by Harry Bertoia. The aluminum spire is by Theodore J. Roszak.

Brick is red; narthex glass is leaded, gray antique.

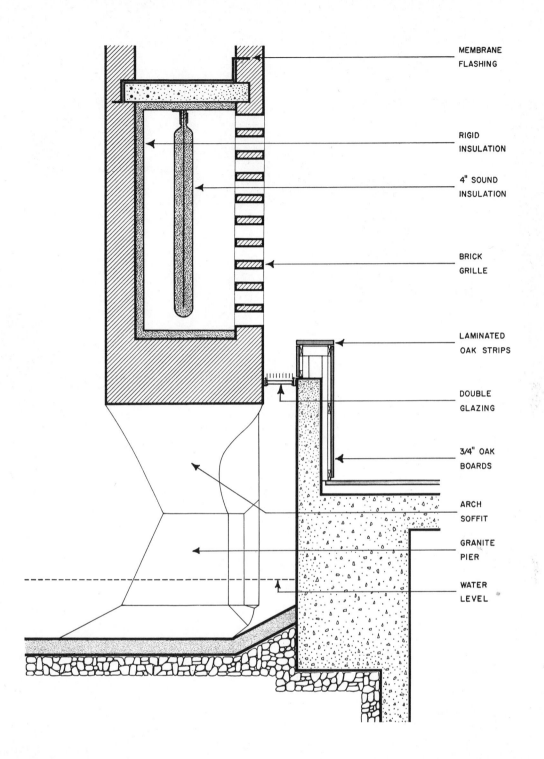

MEMBRANE
FLASHING

RIGID
INSULATION

4" SOUND
INSULATION

BRICK
GRILLE

LAMINATED
OAK STRIPS

DOUBLE
GLAZING

3/4" OAK
BOARDS

ARCH
SOFFIT

GRANITE
PIER

WATER
LEVEL

Ben Schnall

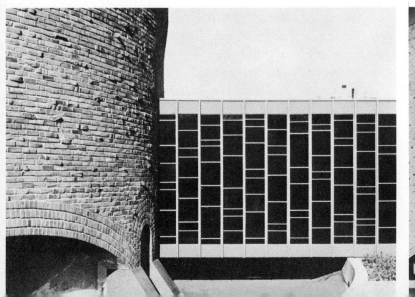

INTERFAITH CHAPEL FOR TEXAS A & M COLLEGE

Bolton and Barnstone, Architects

THIS DESIGN for an inter-faith chapel was submitted in a competition open to former Texas A & M students. The program called for a chapel seating 200, and adjunct facilities consisting of rooms for administration, reception, library and conference, plus a garden accessible from the principal rooms.

The simple enclosing wall effectively expresses the meditative and worship functions of this building which was designed for a site on the busy Texas campus. The central outdoor meditation area is partially covered with a Plexiglas filled steel framework and paved with alternating rectangles of brick and marble chips and stones.

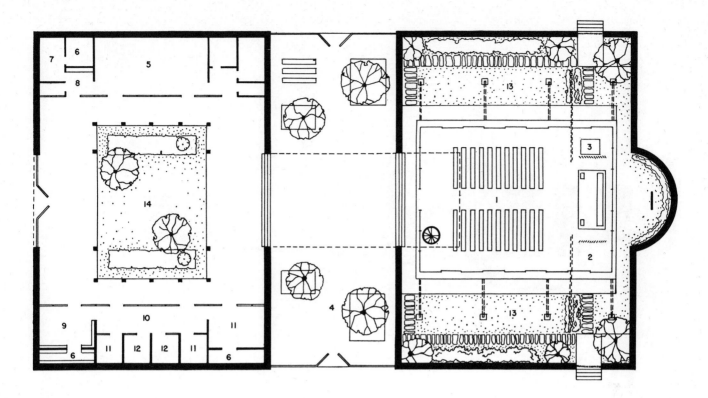

1 NAVE
2 ROBING RM.
3 ORGAN
4 OUTSIDE MEDITATION
 AREA
5 RECEPTION
6 STORAGE
7 MECH EQUIPMENT
8 KITCHEN
9 LIBRARY
10 WAITING-
 SECRETARY
11 CONFERENCE
12 OFFICE
13 GARDEN
14 PATIO

10

FROM THE ARCHITECT: In the near vicinity of the campus are churches of many denominations and faiths which provide religious services, educational facilities and fellowship to meet the choice of Christian and Jewish students. It is not intended that this Chapel shall provide the services furnished by those churches or supplant their importance in the community; but rather this shall be a place where men of all faiths shall find wholesome and inspirational environment for a moment of meditation and communion with God. Its purpose is to provide space for quiet meditation and discussion, a garden for beauty and enjoyment, an intimate and memorable sanctuary for personal religious services, rites and ceremonies.

The gardens to either side of the nave are enclosed and made private by the brick walls and create a feeling of security and beauty. The choir loft is above on a projected balcony and may be used as auxiliary seating.

The court between the nave and the administrative area serves as circulation — as a place for occasional outside worship and as emphasis to the separate character of the Chapel and the administrative parts. Central to the entire design is the use of the garden courts. They provide the means of both extending and unifying the space visually.

Chapel roof framing is steel bents and purlins with steel joists in the administrative portion. Exterior walls of the chapel are glass on all four sides; cavity brick elsewhere in the building. Interior walls include sandblasted glass where facing the court. Roof of the chapel proposes wood decking and shingles; of the flat areas — 5 ply built-up roof. Ceiling is sound-absorbing plaster. Contemplated heating is through natural gas boiler, radiant system with copper tubing. Cooling is to be through 50 ton electrically operated plant with circulating lines to chilled water converters.

Cost (estimated): $200,000
Area: (Enclosed) 6,834 sq ft
(Covered) 5,090 sq ft
(Nave) 83,952 cu ft
(Adm. Fac.) 45,920 cu ft

A RELIGIOUS ARCHITECTURE FOR TODAY

By John Stewart Detlie, A.I.A.

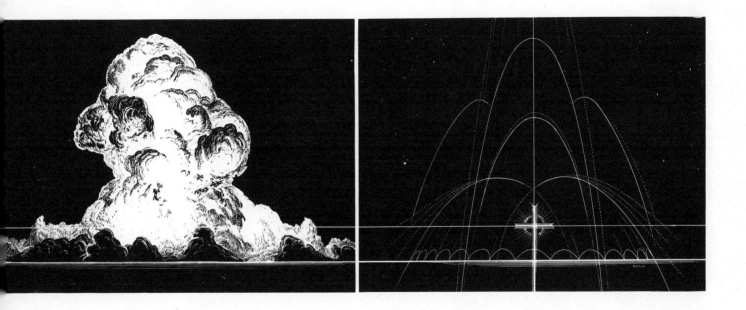

As A SYMBOL of man's relation to the mystery of his creation and of his role in an unfolding universe, the religious building has a special significance for the life and time which produce it. Each age sees that relationship in the context of its own day and expresses it in its arts and architecture in its own way. What of our age? What is the context of our day? Of what are our religious symbols the symbol? If we are to design structures which can stand as symbols of the faith, of whatever denomination, of our day, we must look for the answers to these questions in a more complete understanding of religious architecture, not only from the viewpoint of philosophy but in the context of history, of religion and of architecture itself.

Although each age regards itself as unique, ours has for us a challenge of a new, awesome dimension. We can no longer take the future for granted, and history offers little precedent for meeting this challenge. Where yesterday quantum mechanics and relativity provided the last word in the search for philosophic truth, today a

John Stewart Detlie is a partner in the Seattle, Washington, firm of Young, Richardson, Carleton & Detlie, Architects and Engineers. He is past president, Washington State chapter, A.I.A., and president of the newly organized Allied Arts of Seattle.

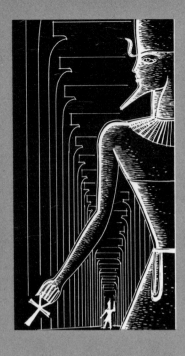

Egyptian

Greco-Roman

Early Christian

new metaphysics suggests that, just as the material universe is revealed, so is man's stewardship of that universe. Yesterday we could comfortably contemplate a pre-ordained universe unfolding in its pre-formed pattern; today we are confronted with fateful choice, and choose we must: either materialistically, interpreting the universe mechanically and denying the possibility of further choice, or spiritually, believing that we are created in love, not by a caprice of history, and that the choice of salvation by redemption is ours to make. This seems the mood of our anxious time, the context of our day. The architecture of religious structures for centuries will reflect the choice which we as a nation make, for we must choose collectively as well as individually, and who does not sense the gravity of our national and international acts?

The Context of History

History as interpreted in the architecture of its various periods is not without its message for us; sometimes clear, sometimes obscure, its record is everywhere eloquent. To understand it, however, we must try, difficult though it may be, to see the archaeological remains of the religious structures of the past in the context of their day, for only in that light are they to be understood.

Just as the simple pantheistic beliefs of prehistoric man are clearly evident in his bold stone monuments and sensitive cave paintings, so is the gloomy concern of the Egyptian plain in the great temples and tombs which, impelled by his religious belief that the body must survive if the soul is to attain a future state, he built of stone or hewed from rock to bridge the inescapable abyss between himself and eternity.

The portable Ark of the Hebrew which enabled him to take with him the tablets of the sacred law wherever he went in his wandering became when he settled in one place the focal point of his religion. In the rich materials with which he clothed his temple in the altar of sacrifice, necessary for the cleansing atonement, placed in the courtyard outside and in the Holy of Holies which contained the Ark, the Hebrew — thousands of years ago as now — expressed his devotion to the one God, Jehovah, the self-existent and eternal.

Greek temples, and later those of their conquerors the Romans, speak in the completeness of their design, in perfection of form and careful balance between movement and repose refined from centuries of search, of the Greek preoccupation with the finite ideal, the tangible reality, the pure present.

It is difficult for a Christian to remember that in its earliest days Christianity was an obscure religion; that although it spread quickly to many parts of the then-known world, its followers were frequently persecuted; and that a public expression of its doctrine of love and redemption was not possible for centuries. For as a Christian I cannot help believing that Christianity, of all the Western world's religions, has evoked the richest, most exalting of our architectural expressions; for it the finest concepts in art, architecture and structure have been evolved; and through it has come to us the religious and cultural heritage which the twilight of the Dark Ages might otherwise have blotted out.

At first without even an established place to worship, this revolutionary new religion adopted, converted and used instead of destroying and liquidating the vacated pagan temple and the basilica of the decaying Roman law court. Even when it could build its own buildings and explore new forms, the basilica remained the essential form for the Christian church, for one of its outward signs was and is the Christian community, the assemblage of the faithful; the basilica, appropriately, was a place for assembly.

In the East the sister church found another and perhaps more natural expression in the dome lightly poised over space like the sky vault over the desert, and in the scintillating gold mosaic decoration of Byzantium.

Despite the invasion by barbarians and the confusion and disruption that followed, a new style — Romanesque — was developing, to be fulfilled four hundred years later in the Gothic style. Geometric, round-arched, solid-walled, with a feeling for sculptural form, remembering the past but strongly of its own time, Romanesque architecture was a material representation of the medieval mind: slow, deliberate, fortress-like, feudal, often devout, patiently awaiting a later fulfillment.

From the East an explosive force shattered the half-sleep of the West. A young Arab, Mohammed, founded a religion which owed much to both Judaism and Christianity but was different enough from either to become the major cause of the Crusades, the great religious wars of the Middle Ages. Mohammedanism spread through Persia, Syria, North Africa, crossed the water to Spain and the mountains to France, its militant followers sprinkling the beauty of their architecture on the land like jewels, from Baghdad to Constantinople, from Cairo to Granada. Lovers of geometry, learned astronomers, inherent poets, the Mohammedans endowed their buildings with a marvelous fusion of strength and lyric poetry.

The second phase of the medieval drama (for which the Romanesque period had been the first) gathered momentum with the reawakening of man's curiosity about himself, about his universe and, at the urging of the increasingly influential church, about his immortal soul. Gothic man, prying into the secrets of the unknown and investigating the entire universe by methods partly scientific, partly superstitious, and burning a sense of anxiety into his nature in the process, opened the way for our modern age of experimental knowledge. Spiritually he felt himself suspended between infinities, between the macrocosm and the microcosm, eternity and the instantaneous, between the hope of heaven and the fear of hell.

All the restlessness, all the turmoil of mind that made the Gothic age a great awakening, became a part of the majestic cathedrals which one by one arose across the continent and in England. Chief among the elements of this synthesis of the medieval spirit was the strength of the faith which made them possible; the devout heart and the stout back, the envisioning eye and the skilled hand, gave of their finest to the glory of God. In the structure tensed for thrust and counter thrust, in the supports soaring upward and breaking into a multiplicity of arches and vaults, in the walls dissolved in gorgeous colored light, in this matchless exaltation of the human heart, medieval man spoke for all time of the aspirations and limitations, the custom and endeavor, the fears and the faith, of his day.

The thirteenth century saw the finest flowering of this spirit. After that century the influence of the church in men's lives lessened and men gave themselves over to secularism, forgetting the essentially spiritual nature of life. The worldliness which swept over Western civilization during the Renaissance has persisted more or less until today. In his "new" learning man "discovered" that he belonged in a "stream of history," and this knowledge, held self-consciously, engendered in him a competitive spirit and caused him to measure his philosophies and his arts against the standards of the classical world.

Renaissance man clothed his buildings with a contrived beauty of form in an architecture of method and expression which, with minor variations, solved all "problems." What he lacked in spiritual awareness he tried to compensate for in size and grandeur, rededicating pagan form in a lusty paean to the power of the church.

But even secularism had its limits. The Reformation kindled minds from one end of Europe to the other, and a reaction to such a stimulus was natural. The Baroque style had its origins in the decline of the Renaissance and the development of the Counter-Reformation; with it, architectural form became an ornamental system which, surging and exuberant, strained to express a mighty hymn of praise and glory.

During the centuries in which the architectural expression of the Christian religion was evolving, Judaism, which antedated it by thousands of years, was a religion in seclusion in the West. Oppressed, often persecuted, sometimes exiled, the Jewish people did not try to develop an architectural style of their own for their synagogues. Instead they accepted the style of the period and of the country in which they were. Nevertheless, whatever the stylistic expression, one basic idea permeated the design: the synagogue was a house of worship. Not until the twentieth century did the Jewish religion begin to find a distinctive architectural expression of its fundamental beliefs.

In any review of the periods of architectural history and the styles of religious architecture (only those in the direct line of Western tradition have been mentioned here) the inner necessity for the expression in ritual and in architecture of the religious feeling of all people is evident. We discern with some dismay that throughout the history of religious architecture many religions and many periods have offered their God or gods more of honesty and beauty of architecture, more

Saracenic

Baroque

Gothic

faith and reverence in the building of the church, temple or synagogue, than we have in this, our age of incomparable possibilities.

The Context of Religion

But the historical context is only one of several in which we must see architecture if it is to be truly of our day. In the context of religion and philosophy, architecture must be judged in the same way as any of man's other activities. Architecture is a component of philosophy. The phrase "philosophy of architecture" is often loosely used, but it should have but one meaning: architecture in the service of philosophy — and, we should add, of religion particularly. For in a very special way the architecture of churches transcends that of all other types of buildings and in its service we should make our noblest effort. If we do not, then we do not understand the essential nature of religion.

If a church is not, at least in part, itself an act of devotion, it fails at its very beginning; for even from a mechanistic, materialistic point of view it cannot "solve the problem" of being an act of devotion without there being devotion in it. Devotion is not something to be poured in by ritual; it must be mixed in the very essence of the mortar between its stones. Those who champion the organic concept of architecture, of structure evolving from inner necessity, are caught in the inexorable logic of their own premise. Religious buildings must be built from the inside out, and in this sense *inside* means the *spirit*. There can be no machines for worship.

The object of religious architecture needs neither roof nor walls, but if roof and walls are needed for the congregation, then the congregation must build in a worshipful manner. Architecture is an act of man fulfilling a need; but in the religious view the act is vanity unless there is something in it of the sacramental, something beyond the utilitarian. This sacramental motive is as necessary to the church of tomorrow as it was to the altar of Abraham.*

How can we appraise architecture in its own terms from a religious point of view? Could the method not be first to understand something of the creative process of the designed universe, to see that underlying each level is the purpose and the principle, and that form and structure follow, each part ordered in relation to the whole? To see the economy and unity with which the whole is achieved, the unique variation in each fragment of matter, each part hung upon time like pearls on a string and suffused with such beauty that the removal of a single part mars the whole?

As designers we can look about the universe and sense everywhere evidences of the ordering process. Material is not distributed through the cosmos like a weak gelatine, formless, energyless, static. Everywhere the hand and spirit of the Designer have been at work and, in all matter, form as shape, effect or formula is evidence of a

* Ed. Note: *Perhaps the historic lack of a distinctive style for Jewish temples and synagogues is an expression of the great importance of the Ark of the Covenant — once portable, still small enough in scale for human comprehension — and the lesser importance of shelter for the congregation.*

greater Architect than any of us. The very stones sing their history; timber reveals the cadence of its growth; mortar locks water into stone in obedience to law. Instinctively the designer can feel himself at one with this universe as he marshals the materials of building into a synthesis which he well knows is a second or reordering of those materials, each with its own cosmic design.

The Context of Architecture

In the context of architecture itself — the art of building with strength, completeness and beauty — we must approach the matter of religious architecture with fresh insight. Although millions of dollars are being poured into the construction of churches in this country, only a few works of real beauty have been produced; we must admit that in this age of great accomplishments, of vast projects, of vaunted scientific progress, of material wealth, we trail miserably behind practically every other age in the qualities of religious structures.

In the design and building of religious structures there is a place for humility. It should undergird our every act, but we need it particularly in the realization of our lack of absolute skill and artistry. Nevertheless, what talents and gifts we have we should put boldly into the service of the church.

Architects should take the lead in interpreting the spirit of an age — this is what they are trained for and what they work toward. But to do this we cannot have too much guidance from the past. From the religious viewpoint, a century is touched with a finger and a millenium is spanned with a hand; across the veil of time all ages speak. We must seek, like the archeologist and the historian, to know the inner meaning of man's life on earth and of his efforts at building houses of worship. Our leadership must be toward the development of a form of expression which will be *of* the congregation but which will show it a new dimension in architectural expression, for our churches built today are for tomorrow, and the form of expression must fit the tomorrow.

One of the difficulties which confronts us is our over-abundance of materials. Yet in spite of this abundance there is a growing monotony in the appearance of our buildings; we use the same materials again and again regardless of the purpose of the building.

An even greater difficulty: although we are well into the atomic age, we are still conditioned by the attitude of the scientific age, which views all life and its activities as "problems" to which there are "solutions" if we do enough "research." We tend to approach the most gloriously demanding of all possible commissions in our profession with a mechanically contrived "problem-solution" process. Great works of art are not created by finding the solution to a posed problem, they are created by constant search for the most expressive form, by trial and error, if you will, applied to an end which may not be clearly defined in advance. Our method must be to bring to the task all the skills of the sciences and all the genius of the arts, with sound business practice as a solid foundation for it.

But the greatest deterrent to awakening the architect to the challenge of this anxious age is probably the lack of vision today of the churches themselves. What congregation of church or temple demands that its edifice be witness to the strength and fervor of its faith and stand boldly as a symbol in a perilous age? More often than not in this wealthiest of nations, those elements which carry the strength and beauty of the design are deleted because of cost, or misconception. How often we tolerate effects and finishes in our houses of worship which we would hide in shame in our homes!

These are harsh situations, requiring firm, resolute action. The average churchgoer, even in this age pulsing with the accumulated challenges of a thousand years, is apparently more concerned with his comfortable sitting and seeing than with how his faith was brought down through the centuries and how it is going to roll triumphantly down the years ahead.

Until there are a vision and an acceptance by everyone concerned in a church building project of the challenge of this day, we shall design around the central spirit of the age but we shall not design for it.

We have much to do. No commission can demand our best quite as a church does. We must go back to the fundamentals of design: form, texture, color, line, plane, solid, composition, proportion. Back through the centuries of art to the Cro-Magnon cave paintings and then forward through the centuries of architecture, through the strength of the Egyptian, the vital line and perfection of the Greek, the structural clarity and spatial richness of the Gothic, the splendor of the Byzantine and the song of the Baroque. Back through mathematics and the laboratory for the new structure; back to the natural world, to the flowers, to the crystalline minerals for their wealth of form; back through the history of the faith for the radiant personal expressions of those who shared in it; back to the pew for a little research in contemporary theology. And for a real experience in the exact nature of man and his church, try the most trying of all experiences: join in a campaign to canvass the members for building funds.

We should not be discouraged even though each church building fails to measure perfection. There is joy in the effort. Our task is a privilege, for each church structure is an affirmation of that faith which alone can bring light to an obscure tomorrow.

Illustrations by the author

BIBLIOGRAPHY

THE FOLLOWING BOOKS have been selected from the large literature of this subject in the interest of providing the active architect a simple, working list with the maximum pertinence for today's problems. Hence, most of these books have been published during the past ten years.

For their help in compiling this bibliography, ARCHITECTURAL RECORD is grateful to:

Marvin P. Halverson, Executive Director, Department of Worship and the Arts, National Council of the Churches of Christ in the U. S. A.

Prof. Herbert W. Johe, School of Architecture, University of Michigan

Maurice Lavanoux, Secretary, Liturgical Arts Society, Inc.

Rabbi Eugene Lipman, Director of Synagogue Activities, Union of American Hebrew Congregations

Protestant

Addleshaw, G. W. O. and Etchells, F. ARCHITECTURAL SETTING OF ANGLICAN WORSHIP. Faber and Faber, London, 1948. An inquiry into the arrangements for public worship in the Church of England from the Reformation to the present day.

Briggs, Martin S. PURITAN ARCHITECTURE AND ITS FUTURE. Lutherwood Press, London and Redhill, 1946. Only 84 pages, about one half on the Puritan tradition and the remainder on the future.

Davies, John G. THE ORIGIN AND DEVELOPMENT OF EARLY CHRISTIAN CHURCH ARCHITECTURE. New York Philosophical, 1953.

Pfammatter, Ferdinand. BETONKIRCHEN (Modern European Concrete Churches). Zurich, 1948. Excellent illustrations.

Summerson, John. HEAVENLY MANSIONS. London, 1949. A collection of ten essays on architecture of which the first, an interpretation of the Gothic, is well worth reading.

Watkin, William Ward. PLANNING AND BUILDING THE MODERN CHURCH. F. W. Dodge Corporation, New York, 1951.

Whittick, Arnold. EUROPEAN ARCHITECTURE IN THE 20TH CENTURY (Vol. 2). Crosby Lockwood, London, 1953. Chapters 32, 33 and 34 include developments in Europe, principally in Germany and England, in the 1920's.

Catholic

Anson, Peter. CHURCHES — THEIR PLAN AND FURNISHING. Bruce Publishing Co., St. Louis, Mo., 1948. Excellent reference work.

Msgr. Collins. THE CHURCH EDIFICE AND ITS APPOINTMENTS. Newman Press, Westminster, Md., 1946. This is something like a sacristan's manual but contains valuable data for draftsmen.

Ellard, Gerald, S.J. CHRISTIAN LIFE AND WORSHIP. Bruce Publishing Co., St. Louis, Mo., 1934.

Fortescue, Adrian. THE CEREMONIES OF THE ROMAN RITE DESCRIBED. Burns and Oates, London, 1934. Both books give the necessary background material for ceremonies, the Sacraments, etc.

Guardini, Romano. THE SPIRIT OF THE LITURGY. Sheed & Ward, New York, 1953. This book is the best introduction to the subject — short and to the point.

Maritain, Jacques. ART AND SCHOLATICISM. Scribner's, New York, 2nd edition 1930, reprint 1954.

Maritain, Jacques. CREATIVE INTUITION. Pantheon Books, New York, 1954.

O'Connell, J. CHURCH BUILDING AND FURNISHING. THE CHURCH'S WAY. Burns, Oates, London, 1955. This book contains much matter already contained in several books listed above, but it is valuable for other matters as well.

Webb, Geoffrey. THE LITURGICAL ALTAR. Newman Press, Westminster, Md., 2nd edition, 1938. This is the standard book on the law and design of altars and their appurtenances. Webb was a stained glass painter but well versed in liturgical matters.

Pope Pius XII. Encyclical Letter MEDIATOR DEI (On the Sacred Liturgy). 1948. Chapters 187 to 196. These chapters, more particularly chapters 195 and 196, give the official directives of the Church relating to religious art — they provide the necessary atmosphere through which an architect can get the feel of what the Church teaches in these matters.

Jewish

Braun, Isadore. JEWISH SCHOOL BUILDING MANUAL. Board of Jewish Education of Chicago, Chicago, 1954. Principles of planning.

Kayser, Stephen. JEWISH CEREMONIAL ART. Jewish Publishing Society, New York, 1955.

Kertzer, Morris. WHAT IS A JEW? World Publishing Co., 1953.

Loukomski, George. JEWISH ART IN EUROPEAN SYNAGOGUES. Hutchinson and Co., London and New York, 1947.

Reifenberg, A. ANCIENT HEBREW ARTS. Shocken, New York, 1950.

Steinberg, Rabbi Milton. BASIC JUDAISM. Harcourt, Brace, New York, 1951.

CONTEMPORARY DESIGN. Union of American Hebrew Congregations, New York, 1951.

General

Thiry, Paul and Bennett, Richard M. and Kamphoefner, Henry L. CHURCHES AND TEMPLES. Reinhold, New York, 1953. A well illustrated account of the three groups.

Periodicals

Arte Christiana. Published monthly by Scuola Beato Angelico, Viale S. Gimignano, 19, Milan. Current traditional design of Church regalia.

Catholic Art Quarterly. Published at Christmas, Easter, Pentecost and Michaelmas; official bulletin of the Catholic Art Association, 4380 Main Street, Buffalo 21, N. Y. Mainly secular.

Catholic Building and Maintenance. Published bimonthly by Joseph F. Wagner, Inc., 53 Park Place, New York 7, N. Y.

Church Management. Published monthly by Church Management, Inc., 1900 Euclid Avenue, Cleveland, Ohio. Special church building issues Jan., June, Oct. and Christmas.

Church Property Administration. Published bimonthly for the administrators of Catholic parishes and institutions by The Administrative Publishing Co., Inc., 20 W. Putnam Avenue, Greenwich, Conn.

Das Münster — Journal for Christian Art and Aesthetics. Published by Verlag Schnell & Steiner, Böhmerwaldplatz 10, Munich 27. Church art and architecture, historical and contemporary.

L'Art d'Église — A Review of Religious and Liturgical Arts. Published every three months by Abbaye de Saint-André, Brussels. (English translation.) Contemporary church architecture and ecclesiastical art.

L'Art Sacré. Published monthly by aux Editions du Cerf, 29, Blvd. Latour, Maubourg, Paris vii. Contemporary art and architecture.

Probably the best foreign periodical in this field.

Liturgical Arts. Published quarterly by Liturgical Arts Society, Inc., 7 East 42nd Street, New York 17, N. Y. (Roman Catholic)

Protestant Church Administration & Equipment. Published quarterly by the Christian Herald Association, Inc., 27 East 39th Street, New York 16, N. Y.

Synagogue Service Bulletin. Published bimonthly by Union of American Hebrew Congregations, 858 Fifth Avenue, New York, N. Y.

Your Church. Published quarterly by the Religious Publishing Co., 22–28 W. Putnam Avenue, Greenwich, Conn.

Architectural Forum
Progressive Architecture

ARCHITECTURAL RECORD

Religious Buildings — Building Types Study Number 223, June 1955

Religious Buildings — Building Types Study Number 217, December 1954

Religious Buildings — Building Types Study Number 205, December 1953

Religious Buildings — Building Types Study Number 177, August 1951

Religious Buildings — Building Types Study Number 156, December 1949

Religious Buildings — Building Types Study Number 138, June 1948

INDEX